West of Everything

NEW YORK   OXFORD
OXFORD UNIVERSITY PRESS
1992

JANE TOMPKINS

West of Everything

The Inner Life of Westerns

Oxford University Press

Oxford   New York   Toronto
Delhi   Bombay   Calcutta   Madras   Karachi
Petaling Jaya   Singapore   Hong Kong   Tokyo
Nairobi   Dar es Salaam   Cape Town
Melbourne   Auckland

and associated companies in
Berlin   Ibadan

Copyright © 1992 by Jane Tompkins

Published by Oxford University Press, Inc.,
200 Madison Avenue, New York, New York 10016

Oxford is a registered trademark of Oxford University Press

Library of Congress Cataloging-in-Publication Data
Tompkins, Jane P.
West of everything : the inner life of westerns / Jane Tompkins.
p. cm.   ISBN 0-19-507305-3
1. Western stories—History and criticism.
2. Western films—History and criticism.
3. West (U.S.) in literature.   I. Title.
PS374.W4T66   1992
813'.087409—dc20   91-15571

Chapter 8 is a slightly revised version of an earlier essay.
From *Riders of the Purple Sage* by Zane Grey. Copyright © 1990
by Jane Tompkins, Introduction. Used by permission
of Viking Penguin, a division of Penguin Books USA Inc.

1   2   3   4   5   6   7   8   9

Printed in the United States of America
on acid-free paper

For Stan

Acknowledgments

No book is the product of any one person, but this project has been especially bound up with the ideas and inspirations of others. I now see that my endless handing around of chapters was a way of communicating with people and not just an effort to get helpful criticism. What follows is a shorthand account of the people and books whose lives touched mine as I was working on this project.

Barbara Wright, business librarian at Paley Library, Temple University, introduced me to the novels of Louis L'Amour. She came up after class one night and asked if I'd ever read him. No, I said, and the next week she gave me a copy of *High Lonesome*. I was hooked. But I doubt if I would have thought of writing about Westerns if it hadn't been for books by John Cawelti and Will Wright, which showed me early on that Westerns were intellectually exciting and culturally important.

Several years later the National Endowment for the Humanities awarded me a fellowship. The book I had in mind—which was to include everything from *Charlotte Temple* to Judith Krantz—would still be in the making if it hadn't been for a crucial conversation with Myra Jehlen, who gave me the permission and the courage to focus on the subject of men in twentieth-century American popular culture. A review article on the state of men's studies ("Toward a New Sociology of Masculinity") by Tim Carrigan, Bob Connell, and John Lee introduced me to the scope and vitality of the subject;

Emmanuel Reynaud's *Holy Virility*, Klaus Theweleit's *Male Fantasies*, and Peter Schwenger's *Phallic Critiques* helped frame my thinking; Anthony Easthope's book on men in movies (*What a Man's Gotta Do*) and a lecture John Fiske gave about men on TV provided some helpful examples. Articles on the Western by Richard Etulain and Robert Warshow spurred me on by making me angry; and essays in *Screen* by Steve Neale and Ian Green encouraged me to think about how people identify with men in movies.

The Hite Report on Male Sexuality let me overhear men talking about their sexuality and their emotions, and the same author's *Women and Love* dramatized—intolerably—my own pain at having been cut out of that conversation. In order to make sense of the amount of pain I saw in Westerns (and subsequently in myself), I turned to Alice Miller, whose daring book (*For Your Own Good: Hidden Cruelty in Child-Rearing and the Roots of Violence*) gave me a way of understanding the behavior of the heroes I was describing.

Meanwhile, my husband, Stanley Fish, had started bringing Westerns home at night (I'd managed to grow up having seen very few). The first was *3:10 to Yuma*, with Glenn Ford and Van Heflin. I loved it. From then on, night after night, I watched—all his favorites and more (some he'd seen half a dozen times). This is a great one, he would say; wait'll you see this. And I would watch and write.

I showed what I wrote to colleagues and friends. In fact, the writing went through so many stages over the course of four years that I may not have remembered everyone I depended on for guidance and support. But everyone who agreed to look at my writing helped me by giving it the gift of their full attention. And some who never saw it—Lynn Ikenberry and John Orr—helped me more than I can say.

Frank Lentricchia published the first and ninth chapters in *SAQ*; Melissa Lentricchia edited both beautifully. Lois Potter commented helpfully on an early version of the first chapter. Fred Jameson invited me to deliver it at a conference he chaired and later lent me Tag Gallagher's biography of John Ford. Kathy Rudy provided wonderful encouragement and excellent feedback on the chapters on language and landscape. Catherine Ingraham made me feel great about the landscape chapter and Jonathan Goldberg offered acute criticisms. John Gourlie supplied helpful comments on a later version. Susan Getze's original and probing responses to the chapter on horses altered my treatment of the subject. Susan Willis also read it and commented in an encouraging way; and Bob Gleckner, Elgin Mellown, Ron Butters, and Sandy Vinson responded supportively to a talk I gave on horses at a department colloquium.

Dietrich von Haugwitz and Carol Adams shared their detailed knowledge of animal rights in readings of the chapter on cattle, which is also indebted to the work of Tom Regan, Peter Singer, Mary Midgley, and Stephen R. L. Clark. The enthusiasm of some graduate students at the University of California, San Diego—where I gave an early version of this chapter as a talk—helped me to persevere when other academicians shied away from its disturbing subject. Bob Sherman gave the chapter a thorough going over when I needed it.

Lee Mitchell, Michael Moon, and Bill Maxwell helped me out in various ways with *The Virginian*. Darwin Payne was an invaluable resource on Wister. I benefited from John Seelye's introduction to the Viking-Penguin edition of *The Virginian*, and his invitation to me to write one for *Riders of the Purple Sage* shaped my approach to Grey, as did an article on sexuality in Grey's fiction by William Bloodworth, and course work done by Kary Smout, Glen Wilmot, and Peter Fulton. I am grateful to Eduardo Cadava for reading that chapter when I needed such attentiveness.

John Warnock suggested I go the Buffalo Bill Historical Center in Cody, Wyoming, and later read the chapter critically for me. Regina Schwartz gave me feedback when I needed it at an early stage. I owe the specific form of the last chapter to Rick Hanson, who told me to read *The Last of the Breed*, and also to Michael

Skube, who asked me to review L'Amour's autobiography, *The Education of a Wandering Man*, for the Raleigh *News and Observer*. Various people I have met in the course of writing this book have expressed their deep love and admiration for Louis L'Amour's work, especially Santos Solis and Max Fish, whom I have written about in the epilogue.

Myra Jehlen read the entire manuscript at a crucial stage and gave me the encouragement I needed to continue. Bob Sherman read it just before it went to press and gave me excellent last-minute advice. Stan read and listened to most of it over the years and urged me on and listened to me complain, but mainly he interrupted whatever I was doing to make me watch an episode of "Gunsmoke," "Branded," "Wagon Train," or a Western that happened to be on TV—and wouldn't take no for an answer. Thank you, Stan.

The energy and enthusiasm of the students in the course on Westerns I taught at Duke University and at the University of California, Irvine, gave me faith in the project and showed me possibilities I never would have seen alone. Bill Atwill, Angela Hubler, and Bill Maxwell—all research assistants at Duke—helped me in countless ways, as did Joe Chaney at Irvine. Jane Gaines and John Clum of Duke's English department gave me advice and information about movies. Carl Brandt, my agent, believed that the book spoke to a wider audience than just the academy and helped me to get it published as a trade book. Deborah Chappel, my research assistant, did the index, helped me find the illustrations, dug up references, went over the manuscript word by word, and showed me every conceivable kindness as we saw it through the press. Liz Maguire at Oxford has been the soul of helpful accommodation; it has been a treat to work with her.

But above and beyond all this, the people whose lives have been most integrally involved in this project—from week to week and from month to month—are the members of my writing group: Alice Kaplan and Marianna Torgovnick (since 1987), and Cathy Davidson (since 1989). In addition to reading individual chapters and sections of chapters two and three times, and reading the entire manuscript through more than once, they made me be true to myself, as far as I was able, and for that I cannot thank them enough. Their insights, concerns, generosity, and love are woven into the fabric of this book. Their voices can be heard in its pages and their spirits hover around it protectively. They are part of it in ways no specific accounting can explain. I look back on the experience of writing this book with gratitude for the friendship it brought me. We came to know each other and ourselves through our writing and through meeting to talk about our writing, and the process is still going on.

Contents

West of Everything

Still from *Cahill, United States Marshall*, starring John Wayne
(Warner Bros., 1973).
Courtesy of The Museum of Modern Art/Film Stills Archive, New York.

Introduction

I make no secret of the fact: I love Westerns. I love to hear violins with the clip-clop of hooves behind them and see the cactus-punctuated sky spread out behind the credits. When the horses pound toward the camera and pull up in a cloud of dust, my breath gets short.

Physical sensations are the bedrock of the experience Westerns afford. Louis L'Amour says in the first sentence of *Hondo* (1953) that the hero "rolled the cigarette in his lips, liking the taste of the tobacco," that he "squint[ed] his eyes against the sun glare." "His buckskin shirt," L'Amour says, "seasoned by sun, rain, and sweat, smelled stale and old."

L'Amour puts you inside the hero's shirt, makes you taste what he tastes, feel what he feels. Most of the sensations the hero has are not pleasurable: he is hot, tired, dirty, and thirsty much of the time; his muscles ache. His pain is part of our pleasure. It guarantees that the sensations are real. So does the fact that they come from nature: the sun's glare, not the glare of a light bulb; a buckskin shirt, not a synthetic wash-and-wear. For Westerns satisfy a hunger to be in touch with something absolutely real. It is good that the eye has to squint at the sun, since what the eye craves is the sun's reality.

I often imagine the site of the Western—the place it comes from and goes to, humanly speaking—to be like the apartment in a certain

New Yorker cartoon. A woman is ironing a big pile of laundry—naked light bulb overhead, cats sitting around on the floor, crack in the wall—while through the door of an adjoining room you see her husband, sitting in the bathtub and calling to her, "Hon, I think it's time we took a ride into big sky country." The Western answers a need to get out of that apartment and into fresh air, sunlight, blue sky, and open space.

Don't fence me in.

Not just any space will do. Big sky country is a psychological and spiritual place known by definite physical markers. It is the American West, and not just any part of that but the West of the desert, of mountains and prairies, the West of Arizona, Utah, Nevada, New Mexico, Texas, Colorado, Montana, Wyoming, the Dakotas, and some parts of California.

This West functions as a symbol of freedom, and of the opportunity for conquest. It seems to offer escape from the conditions of life in modern industrial society: from a mechanized existence, economic dead ends, social entanglements, unhappy personal relations, political injustice. The desire to change places also signals a powerful need for self-transformation. The desert light and the desert space, the creak of saddle leather and the sun beating down, the horses' energy and force—these things promise a translation of the self into something purer and more authentic, more intense, more real.

The hero of Owen Wister's *The Virginian* (1902), says in a moment of rare self-revelation: "Often when I have camped here, it has made me want to become the ground, become the water, become the trees, mix with the whole thing. Not know myself from it. Never unmix again" (280). In Westerns the obsession with landscape is finally metaphysical. The craving for *material* reality, keen and insistent as it is, turns into a hunger even more insatiable. "My pa used to say," says a character from Louis L'Amour's *Galloway* (1970), "that when corruption is visited upon the cities of men, the mountains and the deserts await him. The cities are for money but the high-up hills are purely for the soul." The same is true of the Western. Thriving on physical sensation, wedded to violence, dominated by the need for domination, and imprisoned by its own heroic code, the Western appeals finally beyond all these to whatever it is the high-up hills betoken.

From roughly 1900 to 1975 a significant portion of the adolescent male population spent every Saturday afternoon at the movies. What they saw there were Westerns. Roy Rogers, Tom Mix, Lash LaRue, Gene Autry, Hopalong Cassidy. From the twenties through the early seventies there were hundreds of nationally distributed feature films which gave the general population the same kind of experience on a more sophisticated level. Some of these films—*High Noon* (1952) ("Do not forsake me, oh my darling"), *Shane* (1953) ("Come back, Shane")—have become part of the permanent repertoire of American culture. Western radio shows in the thirties and forties were followed by TV shows in the fifties and sixties. In 1959 there were no fewer than thirty-five Westerns running concurrently on television, and out of the top ten programs eight were Westerns (Nachbar, x). John Wayne, the actor whose name is synonymous with Western films, became *the* symbol of American masculinity from World War II to Vietnam. Throughout the twentieth century, popular Western novels by Zane Grey, Ernest Haycox, Max Brand, Luke Short, and Louis L'Amour have sold hundreds of millions of copies. In 1984 L'Amour alone had 145 million books in print.

People from all levels of society read Westerns: presidents, truck drivers, librarians, soldiers, college students, businessmen, homeless people. They are read by women as well as men, rich and poor, young and old. In one way or another Westerns—novels and films—have touched the lives of virtually everyone who lived during the first three-quarters of this century. The arch-images of the genre—the gunfight, the fistfight, the chase on horseback, the figure of the mounted horseman outlined against the sky, the saloon girl, the lonely landscape itself—are culturally pervasive and overpowering. They carry within them compacted worlds of meaning and value, codes of conduct, standards of judgment, and habits of perception that shape our sense of the world and govern our behavior without our having the slightest awareness of it.

This book asks what the Western hero has meant for the way Americans living in the twentieth century have thought about themselves, how the hero's aspirations have blended with theirs, and how his story has influenced people's beliefs about the way things are. For what the hero experiences is what the audience experiences; what he does, they do too. The feeling of being "in a Western"— the kind of experience that is and the effects it has—are what I am attempting to record. Westerns play, first and last, to a Wild West of the psyche. The images, ideas, and values that become part of an audience's way of interpreting life come in through the senses and are experienced first as drama. To comprehend how they've shaped people's attitudes and behavior, to understand them in an intellectual or conceptual way, one must begin with their impact on the body and the emotions.

The first half of this book highlights some of the genre's main features—death, women, language, landscape, horses, cattle—pays attention to the look and feel of their presence, and asks some questions. Why is the Western haunted by death? Why does it hate women and language so much? What messages does the landscape send? Why are there horses everywhere, and why don't people pay them more attention? What is implied by the fact that the raising of cattle for human consumption forms the economic basis of the life that Westerns represent?

Some of the answers are problematic and raise questions about the values to which Westerns have educated us. For Westerns believe that reality is material, not spiritual; they are obsessed with pain and celebrate the suppression of feeling; their taciturn heroes want to dominate the land, and sometimes to merge with it completely—they are trying to get away from other people and themselves.

The second half of the book looks at these issues by studying outstanding examples of the genre that generate the image of the West people carry in their minds: *The Virginian*, *Riders of the Purple Sage* (1912), the Buffalo Bill Historical Center, and a best-selling novel by Louis L'Amour. Though it's the West not of actuality but of representation I'm dealing with here—words and pictures, not flesh and blood—fiction and fact interpenetrate continually when one considers the life of Western writers in relation to their work. Owen Wister, Zane Grey, and Louis L'Amour in different ways all lived what they wrote. And Buffalo Bill spent the last half of his life playing out the first half theatrically.

Unlike most books on the Western, this one treats novels and films together. For when you read a Western novel or watch a Western movie on television, you are in the same world no matter what the medium: the hero is the same, the story line is the same, the setting, the values, the actions are the same. The media draw on each other: movies and television programs are usually based on novels and short stories; conversely, when you read *Hondo*, you're likely to think of John Wayne. So when I say "Western" I mean everything from a comic book or a fifteen-minute radio show to a feature film or a full-length novel. What matters is not the medium but the identity of the imaginative world. Just as you know, when you turn the television on, whether you're watching a science fiction serial or a sitcom, you know when you're in a Western.

One of the things that lets you know when you're in a Western is the presence of Indians. Yet, to the surprise of some, including myself, Indians will not figure significantly in this book.

When I sat down to watch Western movies in 1986 (the novels are a somewhat different story), I expected to see a great many

Indians. I'd written a piece on Indian museums and a long article on how historians of colonial New England had represented native peoples in their work. I was primed. As I watched, an Indian would appear, like the Indian woman in *The Searchers* (1956) who attaches herself to the young male lead. Her name was "Look." This woman is treated so abominably by the characters—ridiculed, humiliated, and then killed off casually by the plot—that I couldn't believe my eyes. The movie treated her as a joke, not as a person. I couldn't bear to take her seriously; it would have been too painful. I kept on looking.

But the Indians I expected did not appear. The ones I saw functioned as props, bits of local color, textural effects. As people they had no existence. Quite often they filled the role of villains, predictably, driving the engine of the plot, threatening the wagon train, the stagecoach, the cavalry detachment—a particularly dangerous form of local wildlife. But there were no Indian characters, no individuals with a personal history and a point of view. There was the buffoonish old man in *Red River* (1948) who wins a set of false teeth from Walter Brennan, and then they trade the teeth back and forth for the rest of the film, comic relief to take the edge off the relentlessness of the drive. Surely that Indian didn't count. Still I waited, but after a while, I forgot.

Confronted, finally, with the fact that I'd left out what everyone assumed was a major element of Western narratives, I began to think back over the movies I'd seen, trying to remember what I might have missed. *Shane, High Noon, Gunfight at the OK Corral* (1961). No Indians. *My Darling Clementine* (1946), *The Wild Bunch* (1969), *The Big Country* (1958). None that I could remember. *Duel in the Sun* (1946), *Wagonmaster* (1950), *Rio Bravo* (1959), *Warlock* (1959), *Man Without a Star* (1955), *Will Penny* (1968), *Destry Rides Again* (1939), *Jesse James* (1939). Again I couldn't remember any Indians, though they might have been there. They must have been in *She Wore a Yellow Ribbon* (1949), but not that I could recall. I tried a different tack.

Images of Indians sprang to mind, detached from any one picture. That yipping sound on the sound tracks that accompanies Indian attacks, the beat of tom-toms growing louder as you near the Indian encampment. The encampment itself—tepees, campfires, dogs and children running around, squaws in blankets. Most vividly, a line of warriors—war paint, feathers, spotted horses—appearing suddenly on a ridge.

But no people. Now and then a weak imitation, like Henry Brandon playing "Scar" in *The Searchers*. It was bizarre. Either I had managed to see seventy-five to eighty Western films that by chance had no serious representations of native people in them, or there was something wrong with the popular image of Westerns. I remembered the Indians in Cooper's novels—Uncas, Chingachgook, Hardheart—ethnographically incorrect, maybe, but still magnetic, compelling. There were no such characters in the movies I had watched. Logic would suggest that in his flight from women and children, family life, triviality, and tameness, the Western hero would run straight into the arms of the Indian, wild blood brother of his soul, but it doesn't happen. Indians are repressed in Westerns—there but not there—in the same way women are.

And when they do appear they are even more unreal. At least women in Westerns are not played by men. At least horses are not played by dogs, or cattle by goats. Faked scenery is more convincing than fake Indians are. In movies about the Roman Empire, real Romans don't play the roles. There aren't any Romans anymore, so Charlton Heston is OK. But when there are thousands and thousands of Native Americans alive, why should Jeff Chandler play Cochise? Why should Henry Brandon play "Scar"? How do you take Charles Bronson and Anthony Quinn seriously, when they're surrounded by nameless figures who *are* natives? An Indian in a Western who is supposed to be a real person has to be played by a white man. The Indians played by actual natives are extras, generic brand; those with bit parts are doodles in the margin of the film. Of course there are exceptions—everyone will think of some. *Chey-*

enne Autumn (1964), for example, though it has no memorable Indian characters, really does attempt to represent the native point of view. But what I have been describing is the norm.

Since this book was written, one movie has appeared that represents Native Americans in a serious, sympathetic way: Kevin Costner's *Dances with Wolves* (1990). Here the Lakota Sioux (played by themselves) are attractive and believable, individually and as a group. They draw you to them, their closeness is palpable—the family you never had, the community you never belonged to—and you know why the protagonist deserts the army to become one of them. Their lives make sense. But Costner's triumph in this respect emphasizes the sad history that makes his film so distinctive.

The absence of Indians in Western movies, by which I mean the lack of their serious presence as individuals, is so shocking once you realize it that, even for someone acquainted with outrage, it's hard to admit. My unbelief at the travesty of native peoples that Western films afford kept me from scrutinizing what was there. I didn't want to see. I stubbornly expected the genre to be better than it was, and when it wasn't, I dropped the subject. Forgetting perpetuates itself. I never cried at anything I saw in a Western, but I cried when I realized this: that after the Indians had been decimated by disease, removal, and conquest, and after they had been caricatured and degraded in Western movies, I had ignored them too. The human beings who populated this continent before the Europeans came and who still live here, whose image the Western traded on—where are they? Not in Western films. And not in this book, either.

While the Western may have been wrongly credited for giving us Indians, its general reputation as a serious representation of life has been vastly lower than what it deserves. People think of Westerns as light entertainment, adolescent and escapist, but there is nothing trivial about the needs they answer, the desires they arouse, or the vision of life they portray. One of the hallmarks of the genre is an almost desperate earnestness. This passage from the opening of *Heller with a Gun* (1955), an early L'Amour novel, exemplifies in miniature the kind of experience the Western likes to put its readers through, and it shows that whatever else they may be doing, Westerns are not getting away from seriousness, or from the demands of hard work, or from living a significant life:

> It was bitter cold. . . .
>
> He came down off the ridge into the shelter of the draw with the wind kicking up snow behind him. The sky was a flat slate gray, unbroken and low. The air grew colder by the minute and there was a savage bite to the wind. . . .
>
> He was two days out of Deadwood and riding for Cheyenne, and the nearest shelter was at Hat Creek Station, probably fifty miles along.
>
> Wind knifed at his cheek. He drew deeply on his cigarette. Whoever followed him had the same problem. Find shelter or die. The wind was a moving wall of snow and the evening was filled with vast sound. (5)

This is a typical opening for a L'Amour novel. A man is alone in a blizzard with a murderer on his trail. Thirty-six hours later, this particular hero rides into Hat Creek Station out of the forty-below weather, having overpowered the man who was trying to kill him. The chapter ends as follows:

> His mind was empty. He did not think. Only the occasional tug on the lead rope reminded him of the man who rode behind him.
>
> It was a hard land, and it bred hard men to hard ways. (15)

The final sentence, in itself a kind of mini-Western, epitomizes familiar clichés. It represents physical strength as an ideal. It says that the hero is tough and strong, that the West made him that way; and it says this in simple language that anyone could understand. But it does not represent an escape from work. The protagonist is caught in a snowstorm, in below-zero weather, fifty miles from the nearest shelter; he is in pain and trapped in a situation he cannot escape except by monumental effort. He is able to reach warmth only through dogged persistence and the exercise of an unrelenting purpose. It is the ability to endure pain for a long time that saves him.

In fact all the qualities required of the protagonist are qualities required to complete an excruciatingly difficult task: self-disicipline; unswerving purpose; the exercise of knowledge, skill, ingenuity, and excellent judgment; and a capacity to continue in the face of total exhaustion and overwhelming odds. At the most literal level, then, the experience the scene reproduces for its readers is that of work rather than leisure, of effort rather than rest or relaxation. Whatever it may be an escape from for its audience, this scene is not an escape from the psychological demands of work.

It is, however, an escape from something else. Though it reproduces with amazing thoroughness and intensity the emotional experience of performing intolerable labor, it removes the feelings associated with doing work from their usual surroundings and places them in a locale and a set of circumstances that expand their meaning, endow them with an overriding purpose, and fill them with excitement. In short, hard work is transformed here from the necessity one wants to escape into the most desirable of human endeavors: action that totally saturates the present moment, totally absorbs the body and mind, and directs one's life to the service of an unquestioned goal. What the reader and the hero feel at the end of the episode is a sense of hard-won achievement. The laboriousness of the experience, its mind-numbing and backbreaking demands, are essential to the form of satisfaction the narrative affords.

Rather than offering an alternative to work, the novels of Louis L'Amour make work their subject. They transfer the feelings of effort and struggle that belong to daily life into a situation that gives them a point, usually the preservation of life itself. In story after story the hero undergoes an ordeal that exacts superhuman exertions. Protagonists crawl across deserts on their hands and knees, climb rock faces in the blinding sun, starve in snowbound cabins in the mountains, walk or ride for miles on end with all but mortal wounds, survive for long periods of time without water, without shelter, without sleep. Although the settings are exotic and the circumstances extreme, these situations call on the same qualities that get people out of bed to go to work, morning after morning. They require endurance more than anything else; not so much the ability to make an effort as the ability to sustain it. It isn't pain that these novels turn away from. It isn't self-discipline or a sense of responsibility. Least of all is it the will to persevere in the face of difficulty. What these novels offer that life does not offer is the opposite of a recreational spirit. It is seriousness. They posit effort and perseverance not only as necessary to salvation but as salvation itself. It is when your own life doesn't require of you the effort, concentration, and intensity of aim that L'Amour's heroes need to stay alive that you want to be out with them in a Wyoming blizzard with a murderer on your trail fifty miles from Hat Creek Station.

The desire to test one's nerve, physically, as a means of self-fulfillment is illustrated in a somewhat prosaic but nevertheless telling way in a joke someone sent in to *Reader's Digest*. The anecdote helps to explain why L'Amour's audience might be looking not for an escape from work but for quite the reverse:

> Last summer my wife and I met a couple at a restaurant. After an enjoyable lunch, the women decided to go shopping, and I invited the man to go sailing. Later, while we were out on the water, a storm blew up. The tide had gone out, and we were downwind trying to work our way back through a narrow channel. At one point the boat grounded and we had to climb overboard and shove with all our might to get it back in deeper water. As my new friend stood there, ankle deep in muck, the wind blowing his hair wildly, rain streaming down his face, he grinned at me, and with unmistakable sincerity said, "Sure beats shopping!"

The men in this joke, like the heroes in L'Amour's novels, are braving the elements. Drenched to the skin, pushing a boat off a sandbar, they are having the time of their lives. They enjoy themselves so much not because they are out on a pleasure trip but because they are meeting a challenge, a challenge whose value is defined by contrast with the activity the women are engaged in—shopping. Shopping, in this context, not only implies nonmale activity, it embodies everything that readers of Westerns are trying to get away from: triviality, secondariness, meaningless activity. That the qualities devalued here are associated with women is essential to the way Westerns operate as far as gender is concerned. Requiring no effort of the will, no test of strength or nerve, shopping is seen here as petty and inconsequential; whatever paltry resources it calls on, however it is performed, shopping makes no difference. It isn't serious.

Ordinary work—in fact, ordinary life—is too much like shopping. It never embodies what the hero's struggle to get out of the blizzard embodies: the fully saturated moment. But this is not because life in the twentieth century involves people in all those transactions the Western hero traditionally rejects—the acquisition of material goods, the desire for social status, the search for luxuries. What Westerns criticize in daily life is not the presence of things, technology, laws, or institutions per se, but the sense that life under these conditions isn't going anywhere. If Westerns seem to long for the out-of-doors, for a simplified social existence, for blizzards and shoot-outs and fabulous exploits, it isn't because their readers want to give up TV and computers and fast foods and go back to life on the frontier. It's that life on the frontier is a way of imagining the self in a boundary situation—a place that will put you to some kind of ultimate test. What distinguishes the life of the L'Amour hero from that of his readers isn't that he can build a fire in the snow, kill ten bandits with six bullets, or get on his horse and ride out of town whenever he wants to; it is that he never fritters away his time. Whatever he does, he gives it everything he's got because he's always in a situation where everything he's got is the necessary minimum.

In the foreword to the thirtieth-anniversary edition of *Hondo*, his most famous novel, L'Amour declares that working people are not only his intended audience but the subjects of his stories as well:

I sing of arms and men, not of presidents, kings, generals, and passing explorers, but of those who survived their personal, lonely Alamos, men who drove the cattle, plowed the furrows, built their shelters against the wind, the men who built a nation. (vi)

L'Amour's epic description of life in the Old West suggests that the hunger Westerns satisfy is a hunger not for adventure but for meaning. What these books offer their readers is not free time but its very antithesis: pressure so acute that time disappears. The trouble with ordinary work isn't, as people generally assume, that it demands too much of you but that it doesn't demand enough. F. O. Matthiessen once wrote of Herman Melville that his novels called the whole soul of man into being; that is what, in their way, the novels of Louis L'Amour aim to do.

The whole soul of man. "Man?" What about woman?

When they speak of their youthful afternoons at the movies, the men I talk to invariably have a certain ruminative tone in their voices, smiling inwardly at something I can't see. "Every Saturday," they say, "for years, I used to go . . . " and then they mention some (to me) extraneous circumstance, like how much they paid, or the name of the movie theater, or what they used to eat. Then, invariably, they list the names of the heroes—Roy Rogers, Gene Autry, Tom Mix, Lash LaRue; they try to remember them all, as if they were baseball statistics—and sometimes say which one they liked best. They pronounce these names like the words to a prayer whose meaning they have forgotten, and trail off into a silence I used to think was significant but which may be just a nostalgic blur. Or it may be full of things they can't articulate. These conversations, at any rate, are maddening. Here am I trying *manfully* to write about Westerns, starting from zero and getting bleary-eyed in the process, and there they are with this huge backlog of knowledge and experience to draw on—I'll never catch up—from which they draw nothing but a list of names.

With women it's different. Either you draw a blank when you ask them about Westerns or you get something less formulaic and more personal. When they do have a history with the genre, women are split into two camps: those who identified with the hero and those who didn't or couldn't. Annie Oakley and Dale Evans were for this second group. One friend said she loved "Bonanza" so much that she had to invent a female character so that she could participate as a woman, and spent a long time deciding whether to be the fourth wife or one of the Cartwright children. Another friend told me she could identify with male heroes but only the nonwhite, non-WASP ones, Tonto and Zorro. Another was so crazy about Gene Autry as a child that she wore guns around all the time and for two years refused to answer to anything but "Gene." I identified with everybody—the Lone Ranger, Tonto, Silver, and, if there was a woman in the story, with her, too, though sometimes she was just too different from the men to be anybody I'd want to be.

I used to listen to "The Lone Ranger" on the radio on Monday, Wednesday, and Friday evenings at seven-fifteen. I loved the sound of hoofbeats and the *William Tell* Overture, the nasal intonation of the Lone Ranger's voice when he spoke to Tonto, the cry "Hi-ho, Silver, away!" But I wasn't really a fan. It wasn't the Lone Ranger or Gene Autry who laid the groundwork for my later love of Westerns, it was horses. From the age of eight to about thirteen, I was horse-crazy. I lived for the summers when I took riding lessons, wanted my parents to buy me a horse, fantasized about horses, drew pictures of them, read books about them, collected statues of them, pretended to *be* a horse.

Up comes the inevitable Freudian query: horse as penis? I don't know. To me, at age eight, a penis was an embarrassing-looking thing that hung down between a boy's legs. *I* certainly didn't want one. But horses and riding were my experience of happiness and freedom. Horses smelled good and made me feel physically alive. Riding showed me that right effort could be followed by accomplishment, made me feel competent, and gave me an experience of risk and daring that I craved. It was the best thing life had to offer.

With late adolescence this enthusiasm wore off, and it wasn't until I was almost forty that I read my first L'Amour novel. But as soon as I did I was back in the saddle again. This time I fell in with the heroes. They worked hard, and so did I. They kept going under adverse circumstances, and so did I. Often, after finishing a L'Amour book, I would feel inspired to go back to some difficult task, strengthened in the belief that I could complete it if only I didn't give up. Westerns made me want to work, they made me feel good about working, they gave me what I needed in order to work hard.

So although Westerns have traditionally been fare for men and not for women, women can feel engaged by them. In fact, since stories about men (at least in our culture) function as stories about all people, women learn at an early age to identify with male heroes. Socialized to please others, women also acquire early on the ability to sympathize with people whose circumstances are different from their own. Hence they regularly identify across gender lines in reading and in watching movies and television.

Feminist theorists have shown how movies force women to look at women from the point of view of men, seeing women as sex objects, forcing women to identify against themselves in order to participate in the story. Westerns do this more than most narratives, and the attitudes toward oneself that form over a lifetime of seeing oneself trivialized and degraded are extremely difficult to undo. But in the very act of harming women in this way Westerns also force men into parts that are excruciating to perform, parts that, given the choice, they probably would not have wanted to play.

In fact, what is most interesting about Westerns at this moment in history is their relation to gender, and especially the way they created a model for men who came of age in the twentieth century. The model was not for women but for men: Westerns insist on this point by emphasizing the importance of manhood as an ideal. It is not one ideal among many, it is *the* ideal, certainly the only one worth dying for. It doesn't matter whether a man is a sheriff or an outlaw, a rustler or a rancher, a cattleman or a sheepherder, a miner or a gambler. What matters is that he be a *man.* That is the only side to be on. The most poignant expression of this sentiment, so characteristic of the genre, comes in the late, and in many ways uncharacteristic, film *The Wild Bunch.* Robert Ryan, leader of a gang of louts hired by the railroad to catch a gang of thieves to which he used to belong, has just heard one of his crew say something derogatory about the gang they're chasing. And he replies, "We're after *men,* and I wish to God I was with them."

That, I think, is the way the audience of a Western feels when things are going right. "I wish to God I was with them." I feel that way a lot when I watch Westerns, and sometimes I feel exactly the reverse.

I am simultaneously attracted and repelled by the power of Western heroes, the power that men in our society wield. I've been jealous of power, and longed for it, wanted the experiences that accompany it, and seen the figures who embody it as admirable, worthy to emulate, and sexually attractive. I have also been horrified by the male exercise of power and, like most women, have felt victimized by it in my own life. In a sense my engagement with the Western has been an attempt to understand why men act the way they do and to come to terms with it emotionally.

So I came to this project with a mixture of motives, not unlike the motives with which men originally came to the West: curiosity, awe, and a desire to subdue and possess. There was the feeling that if I could understand what made these Western heroes so attractive, I could gain some advantage over men, turn the knowledge against them when I needed to. In a sense, I suppose, I wanted to do to Western heroes what my own culture, in the form of Western novels and movies, had done to women, had done to me. I wanted to hold men up to scorn.

But though I have felt contempt and hatred for the Western hero, for his self-righteousness, for his silence, for his pathetic determination to be tough, the desire to *be* the Western hero, with his squint and his silence and his swagger, always returns. I want to be up there in the saddle, looking down at the woman in homespun; I want to walk into the cool darkness of the saloon, order a whiskey at the bar, feel its warmth in my throat, and hear the conversation come to a sudden halt. I want these things and I don't want them, because I have found in my own life, and through reading and watching Westerns, that the price for these experiences, or rather, for the power they represent, is too high. The price the Western exacts from its heroes is written in the expression on Gary Cooper's face throughout *High Noon* as he tries to get help in confronting Frank Miller's gang. The expression is one of fear, distaste, determination, and inward pain. It is impossible not to share that pain with Western heroes if one is trying to understand them. Consequently, my attitude toward the hero is always shifting. Outrage, disdain, admiration, emulation, compassion.

A word about pain. Westerns invite their audiences to undergo a considerable amount of it. And for a long time I imagined it was only *other* readers and viewers who responded to this invitation, albeit subliminally. The attraction to suffering, I thought, was a pathology found especially in men who, as a class, were always trying to prove that they could take it. Never did it occur to me that I loved the pain I was describing, and that in fact *everything* I said about the Western hero—and, by implication, his audience— was in varying degrees true of me as well.

Elements of the Western

I

Still from *The Good, The Bad, and the Ugly* (United Artists, 1966).
Courtesy of the Museum of Modern Art/Film Stills Archive, New York.

Death

1

Near the beginning of *Hondo*, one of Louis L'Amour's best-known novels, the hero discovers the remains of a fight between a band of Apaches and a company of U.S. cavalrymen. He sees "all that remained of Company C, the naked bodies of the dead, fallen in their blood and their glory as fighting men should" (56). Hondo muses on the scene of battle, reconstructing what must have happened, noting those whom the Indians had left unmutilated as a mark of respect for their courage. He admires the old scout "who had held out at least an hour longer than the others. . . . He had defeated his ancient fears of loneliness, sickness and poverty" (56).

Hondo continues on his way, taking shelter from a storm in a dugout on the side of a hill. He settles down for the night, thinking of the woman he has just begun to love, and then L'Amour writes this paragraph:

> Somewhere along the tangled train of his thoughts he dropped off and slept, and while he slept the rain roared on, tracks were washed out, and the bodies of the silent men of Company C lay wide-eyed to the rain and bare-chested to the wind, but the blood and the dust washed away, and the stark features of Lieutenant Creyton C. Davis, graduate of West Point, veteran of the Civil War and the Indian wars, darling of Richmond dance floors, hero of a Washington romance, dead now in the long grass on a lonely hill, west of everything. (59)

To go west, as far west as you can go, west of everything, is to die. Death is everywhere in this genre. Not just in the shoot-outs, or in the scores of bodies that pile up toward the narrative's close but, even more compellingly, in the desert landscape with which the bodies of the gunned-down eventually merge. The classical Western landscape is a tableau of towering rock and stretching sand where nothing lives. Its aura of death, both parodied and insisted on in place names like Deadwood and Tombstone, is one of the genre's most essential features, more seductive than the saloon girl's breasts, more necessary than six-guns. For although to die is to lose the game—Lieutenant Davis's apotheosis is only a small landmark along the trail of Hondo's victorious struggle to live—the sense of consummation the description of Company C conveys, their trans-figuration in death, "fallen in their blood and their glory," make them enviable. Their perfection is sealed; they have paid the ulti-mate price and are at rest.

The picture of Company C—wide-eyed to the rain and bare-chested to the wind—embodies the thing that makes Westerns different from other genres where death is also to the fore—spy thrillers, gangster movies, detective novels. Death as represented in Westerns is death under the aspect of nature, of beauty, and of some kind of spiritual transcendence. Though death is what the hero is always trying to avoid, and what we continually escape along with him, death is constantly being courted, flirted with, and imposed (on others) in scenes that have a ritual quality to them. Often, death makes a sudden, momentary appearance early in the story, as if to put us on notice that life is what is at stake here, and nothing less. The imminence of death underwrites the plot, makes the sensory details of the setting extraordinarily acute, and is responsible for the ritual nature of the climax: a moment of violence formalized, made grave and respectable, by the thought of annihilation.

The ritualization of the moment of death that climaxes most Western novels and films hovers over the whole story and gives its typical scenes a faintly sacramental aura. The narrative's stylization is a way of controlling its violence. It is because the Western depicts life lived at the edge of death that the plot, the characters, the setting, the language, the gestures, and even the incidental episodes—a bath, a shave, a game of cards—are so predictable. The repetitive character of the elements produces the same impression of novelty within a rigid structure of sameness as the thousand ways a sonneteer finds to describe his mistress's eyes. Within a terribly strict set of thematic and formal codes, the same maneuvers are performed over and over. Thus, the question of *how* a particular action will take place is just as important as *what* will happen. Half the pleasure of Westerns comes from this sense of familiarity, spliced with danger.

When the Earps and Doc Holliday face the Clantons and the McLaurys in their famous shoot-out in Tombstone, it doesn't matter how many times you've seen it before, the suspense still holds, life still hangs in the balance. Likewise, seeing the same characters do the same thing in a different way each time—in *My Darling Clementine, Gunfight at the OK Corral, Warlock, Hour of the Gun* (1967)—deepens the experience. You feel you have a stake in how the event will unfold because you know the territory. Part of what the scene is about is its difference from earlier versions; every change in atmosphere, staging, timing, and emphasis producing a different meaning. The imminence of death in the story line and the setting generates these repetitions and makes them titillating.

Just as when human beings age they become more and more like themselves, so as the Western ages death comes more and more to the fore, and there emerges an even greater consciousness, at least on the part of Western filmmakers, of the genre's characteristic moves. In *The Wild Bunch, Butch Cassidy and the Sundance Kid* (1969), and, in a different way, *The Shootist* (1976), death becomes the central focus: the death of the Old West, the deaths of the main characters, and the impending death of the

Still from *Blood on the Moon*, starring Robert Mitchum (RKO, 1948).
Courtesy of the Museum of Modern Art/Film Stills Archive, New York.

genre itself. You might say that in these films death is almost the only thing.

Yet *The Shootist*, which tells the story of a gunfighter dying of cancer—played by John Wayne, who at the time of the filming was dying of cancer himself—is not a sad film or even a nobly tragic one. It is bright, light-filled, punctuated by moments of understanding and sympathy which vindicate the hero's way of life and point forward with hope to the future. The absence of tragedy does not stem from a refusal to face facts (facts are what the Western is always desperately trying to face); rather, it stems from an acceptance of death. Death, to borrow a line from Wallace Stevens, is the mother of beauty, in this as in most Westerns. Death brings dignity and meaning as well as horror, and its terrifying presence in the long run comforts and reassures. For death is the great escape, as well as that from which one longs to be delivered.

In trying to understand the Western as a narrative speaking to and for American culture, one has to ask why, at a certain moment in history, a genre should arise in which death of a particular kind should command so much attention. We tend to act as if there had always been stories about men who shoot each other down in the dusty main streets of desert towns. But these stories came into being only shortly after the towns themselves did, and although the shooting stopped a few years later, American culture has been obsessed by that particular scene of violence ever since.

One way of explaining why Westerns became popular when they did is to follow a scholar like Richard Etulain, who attributes the rise of the Western to "the conflict between industrial and agricultural America and the resultant nostalgia for the past"; the ethos of the "strenuous age" represented by Teddy Roosevelt, militant Anglo-Saxonism, and the Spanish-American War; the disappearance of the dime novel and a rise of interest in historical fiction; along with an increased interest in the West (56–60). This sort of account, which is perfectly acceptable on its own terms, exemplifies a *mode* of historical explanation that, to my mind, does less to explain the mentality of the Western than to extend it. By this I mean that the Western, and the larger cultural movements of which the Western is a part, have taught people to see the world in a certain way. We have been educated to believe that wars are important turning points in human history (in this case, the Spanish-American War); to omit women from the historical record entirely, not imagining that women's roles could have anything to do with the rise of a literary genre; to deny the relevance of religious or spiritual experience to understanding human events; and to focus on great men like Teddy Roosevelt, assuming that men are naturally at the center of significant change.

This view of the way history works, applied to the Western, tries to account for its origin in the very terms the Western itself has popularized. For the Western is secular, materialist, and antifeminist; it focuses on conflict in the public space, is obsessed by death, and worships the phallus. Notably, this kind of explanation does not try to account for the most salient fact about the Western—that it is a narrative of male violence—for, having been formed by the Western, that is what such explanations already take for granted.

But if you ask what accounts, at the beginning of the twentieth century, for the rise of a genre pervaded by death and the threat of death, and if you try to hold at bay the assumptions about history that the Western depends on, a very different story of how Westerns came to prominence will emerge.

In 1896 Charles M. Sheldon, minister of the Central Congregational Church in Topeka, Kansas, began reading a story out loud to his young people on Sunday evenings. It was about a minister who, while preparing his sermon one morning, was disturbed by a ringing doorbell. He finds on his doorstep a young man in shabby clothes, hat between his hands, an air of dejection about him. The man says he has been out of work for a long time and wonders if the minister could help him find a job. The minister says he is very sorry, that he knows of no jobs, that he is very busy, and wishes the man luck. After closing the door he catches a glimpse of this homeless, forsaken figure making his way down the walk, heaves a sigh, and returns to his sermon on following the teachings and example of Christ.

This sermon, delivered the following Sunday, is a great success, but just before the service ends the figure of the shabbily dressed man appears in the back of the church. He makes his way forward and asks to speak, assuring the congregation that he is neither drunk nor crazy. He tells them that he has been out of work for ten months and has been tramping the country looking for a job. His wife has been dead for four months, and their little girl is staying with friends. There are a great many other people like him who are out of work because machines are now doing the jobs men were trained for, and though he doesn't expect people to go out of their way to find jobs for others, he wonders what the minister's sermon about following the teachings and example of Christ means to them. He quotes the hymns they've been singing: "Jesus, I my cross have taken, all to leave and follow Thee," "All for Jesus, all for Jesus," and "I'll go with him, with him all the way." He suggests in a quiet, reasonable voice that if the people who sang those hymns went out and lived them, the world might be a different place. What would Jesus do, he asks, about the men and women who die in tenements in drunkenness and misery? At this point, the man keels over, faint from hunger. The minister takes him home, but the man dies during the course of the week.

The next Sunday the minister arrives in church a changed person. He tells the congregation that he has taken a vow for the next year to ask before he does anything, "What would Jesus do?" and to try to act as he believes Jesus would in that situation. He invites members of his congregation who feel moved to take a similar vow to meet with him after the service. The rest of the story, which Sheldon called *In His Steps*, concerns what happens to these people as a result.

In His Steps was far and away the most popular book of its time. There is no way to know even within several hundred thousand how many copies it sold because, through a publisher's error, it was never copyrighted. And as soon as it appeared it was pirated by sixteen publishers in this country and fifty in Europe and Australia (it was translated into twenty-one languages). Sheldon reports in a 1936 foreword to the novel that according to *Publishers Weekly* it had sold more copies than any other book except the Bible. Exactly how many copies *In His Steps* sold doesn't matter. It was stupendously popular. As a type, it resembled the other most popular novels of the end of the nineteenth century—Lew Wallace's *Ben-Hur* (1880), Mrs. Humphry Ward's *Robert Ellesmere* (1888), and Hendryk Sienkiewicz's *Quo Vadis?* (1896)—novels that not only share its Christian frame of reference but make Christian heroism their explicit theme.

I have spent some time sketching the opening of Sheldon's novel because I want you to understand the kind of book it is and the nature of its appeal. Even today, without a supporting context, you can sense the enormous power it must have had. My point is that only six years after *In His Steps* came out and sold like wildfire, Owen Wister's *The Virginian* initiated a narrative tradition so different from the one to which Sheldon's novel belonged that the two seem to have virtually nothing in common. The juxtaposition, I think, helps to explain a great deal about the purpose and meaning of Westerns and, among other things, begins to explain the Western's preoccupation with death.

Death in late nineteenth-century religious novels is neither a problem nor a focus. Whereas in *The Virginian* five characters die and the hero almost does more than once, in Sheldon's novel none of the main characters even comes close. The main problem for these characters is not facing death but facing themselves, for if you believe in the immortality of the soul what you fear most is not death but the sins of your own heart. Sin leads to eternal suffering in the afterlife and constitutes a kind a spiritual death. So death, in this dispensation, has a different shape from its secular counterpart. Not physical death but sin is the thing most to be avoided. Avoiding sin means, for Sheldon and other advocates of the social gospel, following Christ's example by reforming the evils of the world. His characters strive for the moral and social courage necessary to defy convention and so, instead of risking death, risk losing their friends, the affection of their families, their money, their jobs, and their social position. In these stories, the challenge is never facing death, but facing your wife, or your neighbor, or your boss. It's what you do with your life before you die that counts. In Westerns, facing death and doing something with your life become one and the same thing. For once you no longer believe you are eternal spirit, risking your life becomes the supreme form of heroism, the bravest thing a person can do.

The Western plot therefore turns not on struggles to conquer sin but on external conflicts in which men prove their courage to themselves and to the world by facing their own annihilation. This form of heroism has consequences for the kind of world the Western hero inhabits. When life itself is at stake, everything else seems trivial by comparison. Events that would normally loom large—birth, marriage, embarking on a career—become peripheral, and the activities and preoccupations of everyday life seem almost absurd. The Western's concentration on death puts life on hold, empties the canvas of its details, while placing unnatural emphasis on a few extraordinary moments—the holdup, the jailbreak, the shoot-out. The story that results, stripped down, ritualistic, suspenseful, seems to be telling a universal truth about the human condition. But the picture of the human condition from which its truth is drawn leaves nearly everything out of account.

If focusing on death is a consequence of the Western's rejection of Christianity, this raises the question of how and why the rejection came about. Given the tremendous vogue of novels like Sheldon's, it is clear that two thousand years of custom and belief didn't just naturally fade from the cultural scene. What the Western shows us, among other things, is that Christianity had to be forcibly ejected. When the genre first appears on the scene, therefore, it defines itself in part by struggling to get rid of Christianity's enormous cultural weight.

You can see that struggle dramatized fully and explicitly in Zane Grey's *Riders of the Purple Sage*, whose opening scene enacts the passage from a sacred to a secular dispensation. The heroine, Jane Withersteen, a young Mormon woman who owns a large ranch the Mormon power structure covets, is about to watch her best rider, Bern Venters, be whipped by the Mormon elders because he is a Gentile. She turns her eyes to the purple hills and finds herself murmuring "Whence comes my help" (8).

The next thing we know, someone is pointing to the west:

"Look" said one. . . . "A rider!" Jane Withersteen wheeled and saw a horseman, silhouetted against the western sky, come riding out of the sage. . . . An answer to her prayer. (8)

He wears black leather, a black sombrero, and packs "two black-butted guns—low down."

"A gun-man," whispered another. (8)

In her hour of need, the heroine, a Christian woman who dresses in white, loves children, and preaches against violence, turns her eyes to the hills. Grey deliberately invokes the biblical reference, and just as deliberately rejects it. Instead of help coming from the Lord who made heaven and earth, as in the psalm, it arrives in the form of "a horseman, silhouetted against the western sky, come riding out of the sage" (8). An emanation of the desert, this redeemer is not from heaven but from earth, connected to the natural world by his horse and to the world of men by his black dress and black-butted guns. He is Lassiter, a famous gunman whom everyone fears, the savior as Antichrist.

The person he arrives in time to save—Bern Venters—represents the men of the nineteenth century who have been enfeebled by the doctrines of a feminized Christianity. Afraid that Bern would kill one of the Mormon elders she looks up to, Jane Withersteen has symbolically emasculated him by taking his guns away. But after Lassiter saves him, Venters asks for them back in an exchange that advertises the phallic nature of the regime Lassiter represents:

> Talk to me no more of mercy or religion—after to-day. To-day this strange coming of Lassiter left me still a man, and now I'll die a man. . . . Give me my guns. (17)

In Venters, American men are taking their manhood back from the Christian women who have been holding it in thrall. Mercy and religion, as preached by women and the clergy, have stood in manhood's way too long, and now men are finally rebelling. But even though the gun is obviously a symbol for the penis, manhood, in this scenario, does not express itself sexually. Violence is what breaks out when men get guns. "Now I'll die a man," says Venters when he gets his pistols back. Which is to say, now that he can risk death in a gunfight, he can be a man.

When Christianity is no longer the frame of reference—that is, when Lassiter arrives—manhood can prove itself only through risking death. At the moment this shift occurs, the gospel of peace and charity becomes manhood's nemesis; urging forgiveness and turning the other cheek, it deprives men of the chance to prove their manhood by facing death at the hands of an enemy. In place of the gospel of forgiveness, Lassiter installs the reign of an eye for an eye. "Mercy and goodness," he says to Jane at the end, "such as is in you, though they're the grand things in human nature, can't be lived up to on this Utah border. Life's hell out here. Jane, you think—or you used to think—that your religion made this life heaven. Mebbe them scales on your eyes has dropped now" (272).

The speech reads like an answer to *In His Steps*. Where Sheldon told people that if they lived like Christians they'd see it could transform their lives, this book insists that you can't live by Christian love because if you do you'll be destroyed. The truth the novel asserts is that Jane Withersteen's goodness and mercy, the 23rd Psalm from which the phrase comes, and the whole Judeo-Christian tradition it represents won't work when the chips are down. Only brute force will, because "life is hell out here," and all the religion in the world isn't going to change it.

The coming of Lassiter with his belief in brute force signals a major shift in cultural orientation. When he rides out of the purple hills in place of the Lord, Lassiter prepares the way not only for a long line of Western heroes played by Gary Cooper and Jimmy Stewart but also for Hemingway's Jake Barnes and Albert Camus's Stranger. The transfer of power from Jane Withersteen to Lassiter entails a shift from a reliance on unseen spiritual entities ("My help cometh from the Lord") to faith in the ultimate reality of matter ("Give me my guns"), a shift that will manifest itself in the twentieth century's overwhelming commitment to science and technology and a decline in the prestige of religious and humanistic discourse. In Lassiter—godless, armed, and invincible—man, through his domination of nature, truly becomes the measure of all things, and scientific knowledge replaces religion as the truth that will save us.

But Westerns, paradoxically, don't follow the course of modern history by setting technology and science in the place of Christian dogma. Though the genre rejects organized religion and a belief in spiritual power, embracing matter, physical facts, and physical force as ultimately real, its emphasis on proving manhood requires a technologically primitive environment. The Western needs a setting, and a set of beliefs, where strength counts more than prayer. Hence, the hostile territory in which it situates itself, and its continual battle against the incursions of Christianity. As late as 1976, in the opening scene of *The Outlaw Josey Wales*, the Western is still carrying on the fight. When Clint Eastwood sees the homemade cross he has put on the grave of his son fall over, he picks up a gun from the charred ruins of his house (which has just been burnt down by the people who killed his wife and children) and starts shooting maniacally at a tree, one two three four five six seven eight nine ten times, every shot ramming home his rejection of Christian forgiveness as a way of dealing with injury, and promising the audience more violence to come.

Exchanging the cross for the gun is a theme replayed countless times in Western films as part of an ongoing guerrilla war against the church as an institution. Church congregations often appear, literally, on the margins of the screen, or just off camera, in the form of small revival meetings whose only trace is the sound of a hymn—always "Shall We Gather at the River?" to which the answer is implicitly no. Sometimes a church building (or the *thought* of one) is present as the backdrop to a wedding celebration. In *Warlock* the music we hear wafting our way from a wedding is not even a hymn but "Beautiful Dreamer," and all we see of the wedding is a reception where Henry Fonda, playing the new marshal, meets the church organist (Dolores Michaels), who, though she opposes the violence he stands for, ends up falling in love with him. Thus, the church is peripheral even to the matters over which it presides, and these, in turn, are peripheral to the hero's business—in the example cited, Fonda's vendetta against an outlaw gang. In *High Noon*, which begins in church, the movement of the entire film— as if to compensate—is away from the sacramental moment of the protagonist's marriage and toward the apocalyptic moment of his shoot-out, the sacrament the Western substitutes for matrimony. But in ridding itself of the authority of organized religion and the belief structure it represents, the Western elaborates its own set of counterrituals and beliefs.

The need to dispose of the corpses generated by the genre's love affair with death affords opportunities for some of its more laconic put-downs of Christianity, incidents that seem innocent enough but are riddled with metaphysical intent. In *Red River*, as the tyrannical leader of a cattle drive (John Wayne) mutters, with obvious disrelish, an ever more perfunctory "the Lord giveth, the Lord taketh away" over the bodies of men he has killed on the trail, we are supposed to perceive the ridiculousness of believing in a divine Providence that has obviously had no part in deciding the fate of these poor chumps, and to recognize instead the power of one strong-willed, almost superhuman man. This message about the bootlessness of belief in "the Lord" becomes even more succinct in *Cowboy* (1958), where Glenn Ford, another cattle drive leader, about to bury a man who has been killed accidentally, asks, "Does anybody know the proper words?"—and no one replies.

These casual graveside episodes aren't just burying Christianity; they are putting something else in its place. When Glenn Ford speaks over the grave of the fallen cowhand, he makes no reference to a deity or an afterlife or to religious notions of any kind. His speech is deliberately prosaic and uninspired; he says he doesn't know why the man died when he did—it could have come in some other way, a Comanche, or his horse stepping in a prairie dog hole at night. "But," he concludes, "he was a good man with cattle and he always did the best job he could. I hope they can say as much for me some day."

As a substitute for Christian burial, these words convey a straightforward meaning; there is no such thing as God, or if there is, we don't know anything about him. What is real are objects in the physical world (cattle), and what counts is how good one is at dealing with them ("he was a good man with cattle")—not just in any situation, but in the workplace, which is *the* place for doing one's best ("and he always did the best job he could"). In the movie's crucial scene, Jack Lemmon, a tenderfoot who wants to become a cowboy, proves himself by going alone into a cattle car where the cattle are trampling one another and risks his life to pull them upright again. He is joined by Glenn Ford (the cowboy), who proves his loyalty to his comrade in doing so. The incident shows both characters being good men with cattle and doing the best job they can, but it adds something more: the ideal of comradeship. As a wise old codger says earlier in the movie, "A man has to have somethin' besides a gun and a saddle. You just can't make it all by yourself."

The ethic represented by the graveside and cattle car scenes would take a long time to unfold; they are laconic, but they speak volumes. *Cowboy* posits a world without God, without ideas, without institutions, without what is commonly recognized as culture, a world of men and things, where male adults in the prime of life find ultimate meaning in doing their best together on the job.

By this point it is clear that in getting rid of Christianity the Western was ridding itself of a great deal else as well. If we recall the opening of *In His Steps*, the minister in his third-floor study, the shabbily dressed man looking for work, the congregation of rich and important people, the main characters' inner struggles, it all contrasts as sharply as possible with the scenes I have been discussing: Company C dead in the long grass, Lassiter riding out of the hills, Venters getting back his guns, perfunctory prairie funerals. Why does the Western leave so much behind? Why does it welcome violence so much? Above all, why does it jettison the country's most pervasive, deep, and sustaining framework of beliefs? The answer, I think, lies not in "the strenuous age," Teddy Roosevelt, and militant Anglo-Saxonism, but in the cultural order they were re-acting to. That order is represented not so much by Sheldon and his contemporaries as by the popular women writers who preceded them. The social gospel religion Sheldon's work popularized was the descendant and last gasp of the evangelical reform Christianity embodied in the popular fiction of the mid-nineteenth century. The female, domestic, "sentimental" religion of the best-selling women writers—Harriet Beecher Stowe, Susan Warner, Maria Cummins, and dozens of others—whose novels spoke to the deepest beliefs and highest ideals of middle-class America, is the real antagonist of the Western.

You can see this simply by comparing the main features of the Western with those of the sentimental novel. In these books (and I'm speaking now of books like Warner's *The Wide, Wide World*, Stowe's *The Minister's Wooing*, and Cummins's *The Lamplighter*), a woman is always the main character, usually a young orphan girl, with several other main characters being women too. Most of the action takes place in private spaces, at home, indoors, in kitchens, parlors, and upstairs chambers. And most of it concerns the interior struggles of the heroine to live up to an ideal of Christian virtue—usually involving uncomplaining submission to difficult and painful circumstances, learning to quell rebellious instincts, and dedicating her life to the service of God through serving others. In these struggles, women give one another a great deal of emotional and material support, and they have close relationships verging on what today we would identify as homosocial and homoerotic. There's a great deal of Bible reading, praying, hymn singing, and drinking of tea. Emotions other than anger are expressed very freely and openly. Often, there are long, drawn-out death scenes in which a saintly woman dies a natural death at home. Culturally and politically, the effect of these novels is to establish women at the center of the world's most important work (saving souls) and to assert that in the end spiritual power is always superior to worldly might.

The elements of the typical Western plot arrange themselves in stark opposition to this pattern, not just vaguely and generally but point for point. First of all, in Westerns (which are generally written by men), the main character is always a full-grown adult male, and almost all of the other characters are men. The action takes place either outdoors—on the prairie, on the main street—or in public places—the saloon, the sheriff's office, the barber shop, the livery stable. The action concerns physical struggles between the hero and a rival or rivals, and culminates in a fight to the death with guns.

In the course of these struggles the hero frequently forms a bond with another man—sometimes his rival, more often a comrade—a bond that is more important than any relationship he has with a woman and is frequently tinged with homoeroticism. There is very little free expression of the emotions. The hero is a man of few words who expresses himself through physical action—usually fighting. And when death occurs it is never at home in bed but always sudden death, usually murder. Finally, nature, which has played only a small role in the domestic novel where it is always pastoral and benign, dominates the Western, dwarfing the human figure with its majesty, the only divinity worshipped in this genre other than manhood itself.

This point-for-point contrast between a major popular form of the twentieth century and the major popular form of the nineteenth is not accidental. The Western *answers* the domestic novel. It is the antithesis of the cult of domesticity that dominated American Victorian culture. The Western hero, who seems to ride in out of nowhere, in fact comes riding in out of the nineteenth century. And every piece of baggage he doesn't have, every word he doesn't say, every creed in which he doesn't believe is absent for a reason. What isn't there in the Western hasn't disappeared by accident; it's been deliberately jettisoned. The surface cleanness and simplicity of the landscape, the story line, and the characters derive from the genre's will to sweep the board clear of encumbrances. And of some encumbrances more than others. If the Western deliberately rejects evangelical Protestantism and pointedly repudiates the cult of domesticity, it is because it seeks to marginalize and suppress the figure who stood for those ideals.

If you look back over the scenes I have cited, there are no women present in any of them, except the one from *Riders of the Purple Sage* which openly dramatizes what most Western novels and movies have already accomplished and repressed: the destruction of female authority. Repeating the pattern of the domestic novels in reverse, Westerns either push women out of the picture completely or assign them roles in which they exist only to serve the needs of men.

At first, a woman will often seem independent, as in *Gunfight at the OK Corral*, where Rhonda Fleming plays a lady gambler (Laura Dembo), daring, clever, vaguely aristocratic, whom Burt Lancaster, playing the sheriff (Wyatt Earp), wants to get rid of because she's trouble. He ends up courting her, lukewarmly, and in the course of the film she becomes more and more demure— as is suitable for the marshal's future consort. But toward the end, when she asks him to stay with her, he can't; he has to go help his brother, a marshal who's having trouble in another town.

The love affair never goes anywhere and occupies only a small part of the footage because the person Wyatt Earp really loves is Doc Holliday, another gambler and troublemaker, whom he had also tried to get rid of at the beginning of the movie. Thus, the Laura Dembo character is an extension of Wyatt Earp (as she starts to wear high-necked, long-sleeved blouses, she gets more and more like him, a straight-arrow, letter-of-the-law type); yet at the same time, as gambler and troublemaker, she is a screen for Doc Holliday, an alibi the movie supplies Wyatt Earp with so that his love for Doc won't mark him as "queer." Either way, she's the shadow of a more important male. Female "screen" characters, who are really extensions of the men they are paired with, perform this alibi function all the time, masking the fact that what the men are really interested in is one another. Western novels and movies not only tell stories that stem from the positions men occupy in the social structure, and tell them from the man's point of view, but they concentrate on male-male relationships, downplaying or omitting altogether those areas and times of life when women are important in men's lives.

In doing so, they also suppress what women stand for in the culture. Near the beginning of *The Searchers*, after a woman and her older daughter have been raped and murdered and a younger daughter carried off by Indians, Ethan Edwards (John Wayne), who is heading up the search party, is addressed by an older woman who says, "Don't let the boys waste their lives in vengeance." He doesn't even dignify her words with an answer, and the movie chronicles the seven years he and his adopted nephew spend looking for the lost girl. In this story, as in many Westerns, women are the motive for male activity (it's women who are being avenged, it's a woman the men are trying to rescue) at the same time as what women stand for—love and forgiveness in place of vengeance—is precisely what that activity denies. Time after time, the Western hero commits murder, usually multiple murders, in the name of making his town/ranch/mining claim safe for women and children. But the discourse of love and peace which women articulate is never listened to (sometimes the woman who represents it is actually a Quaker, as in *High Noon* and *Cheyenne Autumn*), for it belongs to the Christian worldview the Western is at pains to eradicate. Indeed, the viewpoint women represent is introduced in order to be swept aside, crushed, or dramatically invalidated. But far from being peripheral, women's discourse, or some sign of it, is a necessary and enabling condition of most Western novels and films. The genre's revenge plot depends on an antithetical world of love and reconciliation both as a source of meaning—it defines the male code of violent heroism by opposition—and as a source of legitimation. The women and children cowering in the background of Indian wars, range wars, battles between outlaws and posses, good gunmen and bad legitimize the violence men practice in order to protect them.

Yet at the same time, precious though they presumably are since so much blood is shed to save them, their lives are devalued by the narrative, which focuses exclusively on what men do. Westerns pay practically no attention to women's experience. Nor could they. When women wrote about the West, the stories they told did not look anything like what we know as the

Western. Their experience as well as their dreams had another shape entirely, as scholars like Annette Kolodny have recently begun to show.

Now the question is, Why should this deauthorization of women have occurred? Why are Westerns so adamantly opposed to anything female? What in the history of the country at the turn of the century could have caused this massive pushing away of the female, domestic, Christian version of reality?

The answer to this question must lie partly in a story of counterviolence, a story I will not be telling here: in the violence of women toward men, in whatever suppression of male desire and devaluation of male experience followed from women's occupying the moral high ground of American culture for most of the previous century. The discourse of Christian domesticity—of Jesus, the Bible, salvation, the heart, the home—had spread from horizon to horizon in the decades preceding the Western's rise to fame. And so, just as the women's novels that captured the literary marketplace at mid-century had privileged the female realm of spiritual power, inward struggle, homosociality, and sacramental household ritual, Westerns, in a reaction that looks very much like literary gender war, privilege the male realm of public power, physical ordeal, homosociality, and the rituals of the duel.

But it was not just a literary landscape that men were trying to reclaim. In the decades before the Western appeared on the national scene, the role and status of women in American society had been changing rapidly. The post–Civil War era saw a massive movement of women out of the home and into public life. Aptly termed "social home-making," the movement was inspired by women's participation in antebellum reform activities, which had been centered on church and home. "We hear 'A woman's place is at home,' " wrote Carry Nation, one of the great reformers of the post–Civil War years. "That is true but what and where is the home? Not the walls of a house. Not furniture, food or clothes. Home is where the heart is, where our loved ones are. If my son is in a drinking place, my place is there. If my daughter, or the daughter of anyone else, my family or any other family, is in trouble, my place is there.... Jesus said, 'Go out into the highways and hedges.' He said this to women, as well as men" (quoted in Degler, 281).

During the reform era, millions of women involved themselves in socially improving activities outside the home. Here is a list of the issues they addressed, compiled by two economic historians:

> prohibition of alcoholic beverages; ending prostitution; sterilization of criminals; improvement of prisons; physical education for girls and boys; sex education as a means of ending "vice"; pure food laws and the cleaning up of food-processing plants; child labor; public sewers; antitrust laws; tax reform; public utilities; wiping out political machines; vocational training for girls and boys; good nutrition; free libraries; parks and recreation; protecting historical landmarks; public transportation, and peace. (Hymowitz and Weissman, 219)

This list may seem exhaustive, but to it can be added: working with the immigrant populations in the inner city (Jane Addams and the Settlement House movement); agitation for Indian rights; the founding of schools of higher education for women (this was the era when the women's Seven Sisters colleges were established); the women's labor movement (the forming of women's groups within the already existing unions and the founding of the ILGWU); and, of course, the suffrage movement which ended in 1920 with women getting the vote.

It is true that industrialization and urbanization, factors cited in conventional explanations of the origins of the Western, created the conditions of overcrowding and dehumanized labor that men escaped from by dreaming of a home on the range. And it is true that a huge and diverse population split along class lines needed a classless (if not racially and ethnically neutral) male hero who could stand for "everyone." And it is also true that the militarism excited by the war with Spain and the popularity of survival-of-the-fittest philosophies could be said to have created a climate for the Western. But these standard notions of where Westerns came from refer exclusively to men and men's experience. What I am arguing specifically here is that the Western owes its popularity and essential character to the dominance of a women's culture in the nineteenth century and to women's invasion of the public sphere between 1880 and 1920.

For most of the nineteenth century the two places women could call their own in the social structure were the church and the home. The Western contains neither. It is set in a period and in an environment where few women are to be found and where conditions are the worst possible for their acquiring any social power: a technology and a code of justice both of which required physical strength in order to survive. Given the pervasiveness and the power of women's discourse in the nineteenth century, I think it is no accident that men gravitated in imagination toward a womanless milieu, a set of rituals featuring physical combat and physical endurance, and a social setting that branded most features of civilized existence as feminine and corrupt, banishing them in favor of the three main targets of women's reform: whiskey, gambling, and prostitution. Given the enormous publicity and fervor of the Women's Christian Temperance Union crusade, can it be an accident that the characteristic indoor setting for Westerns is the saloon?

Most historians explain the fact that Westerns take place in the West as the result of the culture's desire to escape the problems of civilization. They see it as a return to the concept of America as a frontier wilderness and as a reenactment of the American dialectic between civilization and nature. My answer to the question of why the Western takes place in the West is that the West was a place where technology was primitive, physical conditions harsh, the social infrastructure nonexistent, and the power and presence of

women proportionately reduced. The Western doesn't have anything to do with the West as such. It isn't about the encounter
between civilization and the frontier. It is about men's fear of losing
their mastery, and hence their identity, both of which the Western
tirelessly reinvents.

Still from *Rocky Mountain*, starring Errol Flynn and Patrice Wymore
(Warner Bros., 1950).
Courtesy of the Museum of Modern Art/Film Stills Archive, New York.

Women
and the Language of Men

2

Fear of losing his identity drives a man west, where the harsh conditions of life force his manhood into being. Into this do-or-die, all-or-nothing world we step when we read this passage from Louis L'Amour's novel *Radigan* (1958), where a woman about to be attacked by a gunman experiences a moment of truth:

> She had never felt like this before, but right now she was backed up against death with all the nonsense and the fancy words trimmed away. The hide of the truth was peeled back to expose the bare, quivering raw flesh of itself, and there was no nonsense about it. She had been taught the way a lady should live, and how a lady should act, and it was all good and right and true . . . but out here on the mesa top with a man hunting her to put her back on the grass it was no longer the same. . . . There are times in life when the fancy words and pretty actions don't count for much, when it's blood and death and a cold wind blowing and a gun in the hand and you know suddenly you're just an animal with guts and blood that wants to live, love and mate, and die in your own good time. (144–45)

L'Amour lays it on the line. Faced with death, we learn the truth about life. And the truth is that human nature is animal. When your back is to the wall you find out that what you want most is not to save your eternal soul—if it exists—but to live, in the body.

For truth is flesh, raw and quivering, with the hide peeled back. All else is nonsense. The passage proposes a set of oppositions fundamental to the way the Western thinks about the world. There are two choices: either you can remain in a world of illusions, by which is understood religion, culture, and class distinctions, a world of fancy words and pretty actions, of "manners for the parlor and the ball room, and . . . womanly tricks for courting"; or you can face life as it really is—blood, death, a cold wind blowing, and a gun in the hand. These are the classic oppositions from which all Westerns derive their meaning: parlor versus mesa, East versus West, woman versus man, illusion versus truth, words versus things. It is the last of these oppositions I want to focus on now because it stands for all the rest.

But first a warning. What is most characteristic of these oppositions is that as soon as you put pressure on them they break down. Each time one element of a pair is driven into a corner, it changes shape and frequently turns into its opposite. It's as if the genre's determination to have a world of absolute dichotomies ensures that interpenetration and transmutation will occur. For instance, when Burt Lancaster, playing Wyatt Earp in *Gunfight at the OK Corral*, declares toward the beginning of the movie, "I've never needed anybody in my life and I sure don't need Doc Holliday," the vehemence of his claim to autonomy virtually guarantees that it will be undermined. And sure enough, by the time the showdown arrives you can hardly tell him and Kirk Douglas (playing Doc) apart: they dress alike, walk alike, talk alike, and finally they fight side by side as brothers. Two who started out as opposites—gambler versus sheriff, drunken failure versus respected citizen, rake versus prude—have become indistinguishable.

Westerns strive to depict a world of clear alternatives—independence versus connection, anarchy versus law, town versus desert—but they are just as compulsively driven to destroying these opposites and making them contain each other.

So it is with language. Westerns distrust language. Time and again they set up situations whose message is that words are weak and misleading, only actions count; words are immaterial, only objects are real. But the next thing you know, someone is using language brilliantly, delivering an epigram so pithy and dense it might as well be a solid thing. In fact, Westerns go in for their own special brand of the bon mot, seasoned with skepticism and fried to a turn. The product—chewy and tough—is recognizable anywhere:

Cow's nothin' but a heap o' trouble tied up in a leather bag.
The Cowboys, 1972

A human rides a horse until he's dead and then goes on foot. An Indian rides him another 20 miles and then eats him.
The Searchers, 1956

A Texan is nothin' but a human man way out on a limb.
The Searchers

Kansas is all right for men and dogs but it's pretty hard on women and horses.
The Santa Fe Trail, 1940

God gets off at Leavenworth, and Cyrus Holliday drives you from there to the devil.
The Santa Fe Trail

There ain't no Sundays west of Omaha.
The Cowboys

This is hard country, double hard.
Will Penny, 1968

When you boil it all down, what does a man really need? Just a smoke and a cup of coffee.
Johnny Guitar, 1954

In the end you end up dyin' all alone on a dirty street. And for what?
For nothin'.

High Noon, 1952

You can't serve papers on a rat, baby sister. You gotta kill 'em or
let 'em be.

True Grit, 1969

He wasn't a good man, he wasn't a bad man, but Lord, he was a *man*.
The Ballad of Cable Hogue, 1969

Some things a man has to do, so he does 'em.

Winchester '73, 1950

Only a man who carries a gun ever needs one.

Angel and the Bad Man, 1947

Mr. Grimes: "God, dear God."
Yaqui Joe: "He won't help you."

100 Rifles, 1969

You haven't gotten tough, you've just gotten miserable.

Cowboy, 1958

The sayings all have one thing in common: they bring you
down. Like the wisdom L'Amour offers his female protagonist
out on the mesa top, these gritty pieces of advice challenge romantic notions. Don't call on God; he's not there. Think you're
tough? You're just miserable. What do you die for? Nothin'.
The sayings puncture big ideas and self-congratulation; delivered
with perfect timing, they land like stones from a slingshot and
make a satisfying thunk.

For the Western is at heart antilanguage. Doing, not talking, is
what it values. And this preference is connected to its politics, as a
line from L'Amour suggests: "A man can . . . write fine words, or
he can do something to hold himself in the hearts of the people"
(*Treasure Mountain*, 1972). "Fine words" are contrasted not accidentally with "the hearts of the people." For the men who are the

Western's heroes don't have the large vocabularies an expensive education can buy. They don't have time to read that many books. Westerns distrust language in part because language tends to be wielded most skillfully by people who possess a certain kind of power: class privilege, political clout, financial strength. Consequently, the entire enterprise is based on a paradox. In order to exist, the Western has to use words or visual images, but these images are precisely what it fears. As a medium, the Western has to pretend that it doesn't exist at all, its words and pictures, just a window on the truth, not really there.

So the Western's preferred parlance ideally consists of abrupt commands: "Turn the wagon. Tie 'em up short. Get up on the seat" (*Red River*); "Take my horse. Good swimmer. Get it done, boy" (*Rio Grande*, 1950). Or epigrammatic sayings of a strikingly aggressive sort: "There's only one thing you gotta know. Get it out fast and put it away slow" (*Man Without a Star*); "When you pull a gun, kill a man" (*My Darling Clementine*). For the really strong man, language is a snare; it blunts his purpose and diminishes his strength. When Joey asks Shane if he knows how to use a rifle, Shane answers, and we can barely hear him, "Little bit." The understatement and the clipping off of the indefinite article are typical of the minimalist language Western heroes speak, a desperate shorthand, comic, really, in its attempt to communicate without using words.

Westerns are full of contrasts between people who spout words and people who act. At the beginning of Sam Peckinpah's *The Wild Bunch* a temperance leader harangues his pious audience; in the next scene a violent bank robbery makes a shambles of their procession through town. The pattern of talk canceled by action always delivers the same message: language is false or at best ineffectual; only actions are real. When heroes talk, it *is* action: their laconic put-downs cut people off at the knees. Westerns treat salesmen and politicians, people whose business is language, with contempt. Braggarts are dead men as soon as they appear. When "Stonewall" Tory, in *Shane*, brags that he can face the Riker gang any day, you know he's going to get shot; it's Shane, the man who clips out words between clenched teeth, who will take out the hired gunman.

The Western's attack on language is wholesale and unrelenting, as if language were somehow tainted in its very being. When John Wayne, in John Ford's *The Searchers*, rudely tells an older woman who is taking more than a single sentence to say something, "I'd be obliged, ma'am if you would get to the point," he expresses the genre's impatience with words as a way of dealing with the world. For while the woman is speaking, Indians are carrying a prisoner off. Such a small incident, once you unpack it, encapsulates the Western's attitude toward a whole range of issues:

1. Chasing Indians—that is, engaging in aggressive physical action—is doing something, while talking about the situation is not.

2. The reflection and negotiation that language requires are gratuitous, even pernicious.

3. The hero doesn't need to think or talk; he just *knows*. Being the hero, he is in a state of grace with respect to the truth.

In a world of bodies true action must have a physical form. And so the capacity for true knowledge must be based in physical experience. John Wayne playing Ethan Edwards in *The Searchers* has that experience and knows what is right because, having arrived home after fighting in the Civil War, he better than anyone else realizes that life is "blood and death and a cold wind blowing and a gun in the hand." In such a world, language constitutes an inferior kind of reality, and the farther one stays away from it the better.

Language is gratuitous at best; at worst it is deceptive. It takes the place of things, screens them from view, creates a shadow world where anything can be made to look like anything else. The reason no one in the Glenn Ford movie *Cowboy* can remember the proper words for burying a man is that there aren't any. It is precisely *words* that cannot express the truth about things. The articulation of a creed in the Western is a sign not of conviction but of insincerity. The distaste with which John Wayne says, "The Lord giveth, the Lord taketh away," as he buries a man in *Red River,* not only challenges the authority of the Christian God but also expresses disgust at all the trappings of belief: liturgies, litanies, forms, representations, all of which are betrayals of reality itself.

The features I am describing here, using the abstract language the Western shuns, are dramatically present in a movie called *Dakota Incident* (1956), whose plot turns in part on the bootlessness of words and, secondarily, on the perniciousness of money (another system of representation the Western scorns). Near the beginning, a windbag senator, about to depart on the stage from a miserable town called Christian Flats, pontificates to a crowd that has gathered to watch a fight, "There's no problem that can't be solved at a conference table," adding, "Believe me, gentlemen, I know whereof I speak." The next minute, two gunfights break out on Main Street; in one of them the hero shoots and kills his own brother.

The theme of loquacity confounded by violence, declared at the outset, replays itself at the end when the main characters have been trapped by some Indians in a dry creek bed. The senator has been defending the Indians throughout, saying that they're misunderstood, have a relationship with the land, and take from the small end of the horn of plenty. Finally, when he and the others are about to die of thirst, he goes out to parley with the Indians. He makes a long and rather moving speech about peace and understanding, and they shoot him; he dies clawing at the arrow in his chest.

In case we hadn't already gotten the point about the ineffectuality of language, we get it now. But no sooner is the point made than the movie does an about-face. The other characters start saying that the senator died for what he believed, that he was wrong about the Indians "but true to himself." They say that perhaps his words "fell on barren ground: the Indians and us." And the story ends on a note of peaceful cooperation between whites and Indians (after the attacking Indians have been wiped out), with talk about words of friendship falling on fertile ground.

Language is specifically linked in this movie to a belief in peace and cooperation as a way of solving conflicts. And though it's made clear from the start that only wimps and fools believe negotiation is the way to deal with enemies (the movie was made in 1956 during the Cold War), that position is abandoned as soon as "our side" wins. *Dakota Incident* is not the only Western to express this ambivalent attitude toward language and the peace and harmony associated with it. Such ambivalence is typical, but it is always resolved in the end. Language gets its day in court, and then it is condemned.

When John Wayne's young protégé in *The Searchers*, for example, returns to his sweetheart after seven years, he's surprised to learn that she hasn't been aware of his affection. "But I always loved you," he protests. "I thought you knew that without me havin' to say it." For a moment here, John Ford seems to be making fun of the idea that you can communicate without language, gently ridiculing the young man's assumption that somehow his feelings would be known although he had never articulated them. But his silence is vindicated ultimately when the girl he loves, who was about to marry another man, decides to stick with him. The cowboy hero's taciturnity, like his awkward manners around women and inability to dance, is only superficially a flaw; actually, it's proof of his manhood and trueheartedness. In Westerns silence, sexual potency, and integrity go together.

Again, in *My Darling Clementine* Ford seems to make an exception to the interdiction against language. When Victor Mature, playing Doc Holliday, delivers the "To be or not to be" speech from *Hamlet*, taking over from the drunken actor who has forgotten his lines, we are treated to a moment of verbal enchantment. The beauty and power of the poetry are recognized even by the hero, Wyatt Earp (played by Henry Fonda), who appreciates Shakespeare and delivers a long soliloquy himself over the grave of his brother. But when the old actor who has been performing locally leaves town, he tricks the desk clerk into accepting his signature on a bill in place of money. The actor, like the language he is identified with, is a lovable old fraud, wonderfully colorful and entertaining, but not, finally, to be trusted.

The position represented by language, always associated with women, religion, and culture, is allowed to appear in Westerns and is accorded a certain plausibility and value. It functions as a critique of force and, even more important, as a symbol of the peace, harmony, and civilization that force is invoked in order to preserve. But in the end, that position is deliberately proven wrong—massively, totally, and unequivocally—with pounding hooves, thundering guns, blood and death. Because the genre is in revolt against a Victorian culture where the ability to manipulate language confers power, the Western equates power with "not-language." And not-language it equates with being male.

In his book *Phallic Critiques* (1984) Peter Schwenger has identified a style of writing he calls "the language of men," a language that belongs to what he terms the School of Virility, starting with Jack London and continuing through Ernest Hemingway to Norman Mailer and beyond. Infused with colloquialism, slang, choppy rhythms, "bitten-off fragments," and diction that marks the writer as "tough," this language is pitted against itself *as* language, and devoted to maintaining, in Schwenger's terminology, "masculine reserve."

Drawing on Octavio Paz's definition of the *macho* as a "hermetic being, closed up in himself" ("women are inferior beings because, in submitting, they open themselves up"), Schwenger shows the connections these authors make among speaking, feeling, and feminization. "It is by talking," he writes, "that one opens up to another person and becomes vulnerable. It is by putting words to an emotion that it becomes feminized. As long as the emotion itself is restrained, held back, it hardly matters what the emotion itself is; it will retain a male integrity." Thus, "not talking is a demonstration of masculine control over emotion" (43–45).

Control is the key word here. Not speaking demonstrates control not only over feelings but over one's physical boundaries as well. The male, by remaining "hermetic," "closed up," maintains the integrity of the boundary that divides him from the world. (It is fitting that in the Western the ultimate loss of that control takes place when one man puts holes in another man's body.) To speak is literally to open the body to penetration by opening an orifice; it is also to mingle the body's substance with the substance of what is outside it. Finally, it suggests a certain incompleteness, a need to be in relation. Speech relates the person who is speaking to other people (as opposed to things); it requires acknowledging their existence and, by extension, their parity. If "to become a man," as Schwenger says, "must be finally to attain the solidity and self-containment of an object," "an object that is self-contained does not have to open itself up in words." But it is not so much the vulnerability or loss of dominance that speech implies that makes it dangerous as the reminder of the speaker's own interiority.

The interdiction masculinity imposes on speech arises from the desire for complete objectivization. And this means being conscious

Still from *Stagecoach* (United Artists, 1939).
Courtesy of the Museum of Modern Art/Film Stills Archive, New York.

of nothing, not knowing that one has a self. To be a man is not only to be monolithic, silent, mysterious, impenetrable as a desert butte, it is to *be* the desert butte. By becoming a solid object, not only is a man relieved of the burden of relatedness and responsiveness to others, he is relieved of consciousness itself, which is to say, primarily, consciousness *of* self.

At this point, we come upon the intersection between the Western's rejection of language and its emphasis on landscape. Not fissured by self-consciousness, nature is what the hero aspires to emulate: perfect being-in-itself. This is why John Wayne was impatient with the woman who took longer than a sentence to speak her mind. As the human incarnation of nature, he neither speaks nor listens. He is monumentality in motion, propelling himself forward by instinct, no more talkable to than a river or an avalanche, and just as good company.

WOMAN That's a pretty dog.
  MAN (No response)
WOMAN Well, it's got a pretty coat.
  MAN (Silence)

The foregoing account of the Western's hostility to language refers to a mode of behavior—masculine behavior for the most part—that has left an indelible mark on the experience of practically every person who has lived in this country in the twentieth century. I mean the linguistic behavior of men toward women, particularly in domestic situations.

He finds it very difficult to talk about his personal feelings, and intimidates me into not talking either. He also finds it very difficult to accept my affection. . . . I become angry that his need to be un-emotional is more important than my need to have an outward show of love. Why do I always have to be the one that is understanding? (18)

When I was married, it was devastatingly lonely—I wanted to die—it was just so awful being in love with someone who . . . never talked to me or consulted me. . . . (23)

My husband grew up in a very non-emotional family and it took a long time for me to make him understand that it's a good thing to let people (especially the ones you love) know how you feel. (18)

The relationship did not fill my deepest needs for closeness, that's why I'm no longer in it. I did share every part of myself with him but it was never mutual. (19)

The loneliness comes from knowing you can't contact another person's feelings or actions, no matter how hard you try. (23)

If I could change one thing—it would be to get him to be more expressive of his emotions, his wants, needs. I most criticize him for not telling me what he wants or how he feels. He denies he feels things when his non-verbals indicate he does feel them. (21)

The quotations come from Shere Hite's *Women and Love: A Cultural Revolution in Progress* (1987). I quote them here because I want to make clear that the Western's hatred of language is not a philosophical matter only; it has codified and sanctioned the way several generations of men have behaved verbally toward women in American society. Young boys sitting in the Saturday afternoon darkness could not ride horses or shoot guns, but they could talk. Or rather, they could learn how to keep silent. The Western man's silence functions as a script for behavior; it expresses and authorizes a power relation that reaches into the furthest corners of domestic and social life. The impassivity of male silence suggests the inadequacy of female verbalization, establishes male superiority, and silences the one who would engage in conversation. Hite comments:

We usually don't want to see . . . non-communication or distancing types of behavior as expressing attitudes of inequality or superiority, as signs of a man not wanting to fraternize (sororize?) with someone of lower status. This is too painful. And yet, many men seem to be asserting superiority by their silences and testy conversational style with women. Thus, not talking to a woman on an equal level can be a way for a man to dominate a relationship. . . . (25)

For a man to speak of his inner feelings not only admits parity with the person he is talking to, but it jeopardizes his status as potent being, for talk dissipates presence, takes away the mystery of an ineffable self which silence preserves. Silence establishes dominance at the same time as it protects the silent one from inspection and possible criticism by offering nothing for the interlocutor to grab hold of. The effect, as in the dialogue about the dog quoted above, is to force the speaker into an ineffectual flow of language which tries to justify itself, achieve significance, make an impression by additions which only diminish the speaker's force with every word.

When Matthew Garth returns to his hotel room at the end of *Red River*, he acts the part of silent conqueror to perfection. The heroine, who has been waiting for him, warns him that his enemy is on the way to town. The film has her babble nervously about how she came to be there, how she found out about the danger, how there's no way he can escape, no way to stop his enemy, nothing anyone can do, nothing she can do. As he looks down at her, not hearing a thing she says, her words spill out uncontrollably, until finally she says, "Stop me, Matt, stop me." He puts his hand over her mouth, then kisses her. The fade-out that immediately follows suggests that the heroine, whose name is Tess Millay, is getting laid.

The scene invites diametrically opposed interpretations. From one point of view, what happens is exactly right: the desire these characters feel for each other yearns for physical expression. Nonverbal communication, in this case sex, is entirely appropriate. But the scene gets to this point at the woman's expense.

Tess is the same character who, earlier in the film, had been shot by an arrow and had it removed without batting an eyelash, had seduced the young man with her arm in a sling, and had refused a proposition from his enemy. In this scene she is totally undercut.

As her useless verbiage pours out, she falls apart before our eyes, a helpless creature who has completely lost control of herself and has to beg a man to stop her.

> When I feel insecure, I need to talk about things a lot. It sometimes worries me that I say the same things over and over. (19)

> I can be an emotional drain on my husband if I really open up. (19)

Hite notes that women feel ashamed of their need to talk, blaming themselves and making excuses for the silence of men. "My husband grew up in a very non-emotional family." The heroine of *Red River* cares so much about the hero that her words pour out in a flood of solicitude. But instead of seeing this as a sign of love, the film makes her anxiety look ridiculous and even forces *her* to interpret it this way.

Tess Millay's abject surrender to the hero's superiority at the end of *Red River* is a supreme example of woman's introjection of the male attitude toward her. She sees herself as he sees her, silly, blathering on about manly business that is none of her concern, and beneath it all really asking for sex. The camera and the audience identify with the hero, while the heroine dissolves into a caricature of herself. Sex joins here with blood and death and a cold wind blowing as the only true reality, extinguishing the authority of women and their words.

Someone might argue that all the Western is doing here is making a case for nonverbal communication. If that were true, so much the better. But, at least when it comes to the relations between men and women, the Western doesn't aim to communicate at all. The message, in the case of Tess Millay, as in the case of women in Westerns generally, is that there's nothing *to* them. They may seem strong and resilient, fiery and resourceful at first, but when push comes to shove, as it always does, they crumble. Even Marian, Joe Starret's wife in *Shane*, one of the few women in Western films

Still from *Red River*, starring John Wayne and Joanne Dru (United Artists, 1948).
Courtesy of the Museum of Modern Art/Film Stills Archive, New York.

who, we are made to feel, is also substantial as a person, dissolves into an ineffectual harangue at the end, unsuccessfully pleading with her man not to go into town to get shot. When the crunch comes, women shatter into words.

A classic moment of female defeat appears in Owen Wister's *The Virginian*, which set the pattern for the Western in the twentieth century. In the following passage, Molly, the heroine, is vanquished by the particular form of male silence that her cowboy lover practices. The Virginian has just passed his mortal enemy on the road with drawn pistol and without a word. But when Molly tries to get him to talk about it and "ventures a step inside the border of his reticence," he turns her away:

She looked at him, and knew that she must step outside his reticence again. By love and her surrender to him their positions had been exchanged. . . . She was no longer his half-indulgent, half-scornful superior. Her better birth and schooling that had once been weapons to keep him at a distance, to bring her off victorious in their encounters, had given way before the onset of the natural man himself. She knew her cow-boy lover, with all that he lacked, to be more than ever she could be, with all that she had. He was her worshipper still, but her master, too. Therefore now, against the baffling smile he gave her, she felt powerless. (256)

Wister makes explicit the connection between the Virginian's mastery over Molly and his reticence, his conversational droit du seigneur. Like L'Amour, Wister sees the relationship between men and women as a version of the East–West, parlor–mesa, word–deed opposition. Molly is identified by her ties to the East, her class background, her education, but most of all by her involvement in language. Words are her work and her pleasure and the source of her power. She teaches them in school and keeps company with them in books, but they cannot protect her from "the onset of the natural man himself." The man's sheer physical presence is stronger than language, and so words are finally the sign of Molly's—and all women's—inferiority.

This is what lies behind the strange explanation the Virginian offers Molly of his relationship to the villain, Trampas. He says that he and Trampas just lie in wait for each other, hating each other in silence, always ready to draw. Then he tells a story about a women's temperance meeting he once overheard while staying at a hotel. "Oh, heavens. Well, I couldn't change my room and the hotel man, he apologized to me next mawnin'. Said it didn't surprise him the husbands drank some" (259). Then, reverting to himself and Trampas, the Virginian remarks, "We were not a bit like a temperance meetin'" (259).

The temperance ladies talk and talk; that is *all* they do. It never comes to shooting. Meanwhile, they drive their husbands crazy with their cackle. Drive them to drink, which dulls the feelings men can't talk about. So the Virginian and Trampas (the enemy he passes on the road) hardly exchange a word. They cannot communicate; therefore, they will kill each other someday. Their silence signals their seriousness, their dignity and reality, and the inevitability of their conflict. Silence is a sign of mastery, and goes along with a gun in the hand. They would rather die than settle the argument by talking to each other.

Why does the Western harbor such animus against women's words? Why should it be so extreme and unforgiving? Is it because, being the weaker sex physically, women must use words as their chief weapon, and so, if men are to conquer, the gun of women's language must be emptied? Or is it because, having forsworn the solace of language, men cannot stand to see women avail themselves of it because it reminds them of their own unverbalized feelings? Hite remarks:

> It could be argued that, if men are silent, they are not trying to dominate women; rather, they are trapped in their own silence (and their own pain), unable to talk or communicate about feelings, since this is such forbidden behavior for them. (25)

If Hite has guessed correctly, men's silence in Westerns is the counterpart of women's silence; that is, it is the silence of an interior self who has stopped trying to speak and has no corresponding self to talk to. Its voice is rarely heard, since it represents the very form of interior consciousness the genre wishes to stamp out. But it does burst out occasionally. In *The Virginian* it speaks in the form of a song, roared out by the rebellious cowhands who are getting drunk in a caboose on their way back to the ranch where the Virginian is taking them. They sing:

> "I'm wild and woolly, and full of fleas;
> I'm hard to curry above the knees;
> I'm a she-wolf from Bitter Creek, and
>   It's my night to ho-o-wl—"

The wolf bitch inside men, what would it sound like if they ever let it out? What would it say? The silence of this inner voice, its muteness, keeps the woman's voice, its counterpart, from being heard. It is replaced by the narrative of the gunfight, the range war, the holdup, the chase. By the desert. The Western itself is the language of men, what they do vicariously, instead of speaking.

I used to keep a photograph of the young John Wayne posted on my bulletin board. He has on a cowboy hat, and he is even then developing a little of that inimitable cowboy squint so beloved of millions. But he has not yet gotten the cowboy face, the leathery wall of noncommunication written over by wrinkles, speaking pain and hardship and the refusal to give in to them, speaking the determination to tough it out against all odds, speaking the willingness to be cruel in return for cruelty, and letting you know, beyond all shadow of a doubt, who's boss.

The other expression, the expression of the young John Wayne, is tender, and more than a little wistful; it is delicate and incredibly sensitive. Pure and sweet; shy, really, and demure.

Where is she, this young girl that used to inhabit John Wayne's body along with the Duke? I think of the antiwar song from the sixties, "Where have all the young girls gone?" and the answer comes back, "Gone to young men every one," and the young men in the song are gone to battle and the soldiers to the graveyard. How far is it from the death of the young girl in John Wayne's face to the outbreak of war? How far is it from the suppression of language to the showdown on Main Street? In *The Virginian* Wister suggests that the silence that reigns between the hero and the villain guarantees that one will kill the other someday. And still he ridicules women's language.

The Western hero's silence symbolizes a massive suppression of the inner life. And my sense is that this determined shutting down of emotions, this cutting of the self off from contact with the interior well of feeling, exacts its price in the end. Its equivalent: the force of the bullets that spew forth from the guns in little orgasms of uncontained murderousness. Its trophy: the bodies in the dust. Its victory: the silence of graves. Its epitaph: that redundant sign that keeps on appearing in *Gunfight at the OK Corral*—BOOT HILL GRAVEYARD TOMBSTONE.

Why does the Western hate women's language? I argued earlier that the Western turned against organized religion and the whole women's culture of the nineteenth century and all the sermons and novels that went with them; the rejection took place in the name of purity, of a truth belied by all these trappings, something that could not be stated. But perhaps the words the Western hates stand as well for inner confusion. A welter of thoughts and feelings, a condition of mental turmoil that is just as hateful as the more obvious external constraints of economics, politics, and class distinctions. Women, like language, remind men of their own interiority; women's talk evokes a whole network of familial and social relationships and their corollaries in the emotional circuitry. What men are fleeing in Westerns is not only the cluttered Victorian interior but also the domestic dramas that go on in that setting, which the quotations from Shere Hite recall. The gesture of sweeping the board clear may be intended to clear away the reminders of emotional entanglements that cannot be dealt with or faced. Men would rather die than talk, because talking might bring up their own unprocessed pain or risk a dam burst that would undo the front of imperturbable superiority. It may be the Western hero flees into the desert seeking there what Gretel Ehrlich has called "the solace of open spaces," a place whose physical magnificence and emptiness are the promise of an inward strength and quietude. "Where seldom is heard a discouraging word, and the skies are not cloudy all day."

Still from *Stagecoach* (United Artists, 1939), taken in Monument Valley, Utah.
Courtesy of the Museum of Modern Art/Film Stills Archive, New York.

Landscape

3

Truly Mazzini was right when he said that no appeal is so powerful as the call: Come, and suffer.
Charles M. Sheldon, *In His Steps*

The typical Western movie opens with a landscape shot:

Desert, with butte, two riders galloping toward camera.
Stagecoach (1939)

Cattle on a trail, flat country.
Texas (1941)

Landscape with butte, a wagon train, cattle.
My Darling Clementine (1946)

Desert with wagon train, flat country, a few hills.
Red River (1948)

Flat foreground, river, large mesa on the opposite shore.
Rio Grande (1950)

Desert landscape framed by the doorway of house. Song:
"What makes a man to wander, what makes a man to roam,
what makes a man to wander, and turn his back on home?"
The Searchers (1956)

Blank horizon, prairie, sky.

Gunfight at the OK Corral (1957)

Flat desert, lone tree.

Lonely Are the Brave (1962)

Total blank, misty.

High Plains Drifter (1973)

In the beginning, say these shots, was the earth, and the earth was desert. It was here first, before anything. And the story you are about to see goes back to the beginning of things, starts, literally, from the ground up. In the instant before the human figure appears we have the sense of being present at a moment before time began. All there is is space, pure and absolute, materialized in the desert landscape. "A world of crystal light [as it says in *The Virginian*], a land without evil, a space across which Noah and Adam might come straight from Genesis."

The Western landscape reflects the Old Testament sense of the world at creation rather than the New Testament sense, for the material world is the subject of the Genesis creation story:

> In the beginning God created the heaven and the earth. And the earth was without form, and void; and darkness was upon the face of the waters. And God said, Let there be light: and there was light. And God saw the light, that it was good. (Gen. I: 1–5)

God creates the heaven and the earth and then the light, the constituent elements of the Western landscape. In the Western as in Genesis, the physical world comes first. The only difference is that instead of being created by God, it *is* God.

It is the Alpha and the Omega. If the opening shot recalls the earth at creation—solids rising from a level plain bathed in a pristine light—it foreshadows the end of things as well. The desert is the landscape of death. In *High Plains Drifter*, for example, the protagonist, who is in fact dead, appears from out of a misty blank in an opening shot that blends sky and earth into an originary unity and, when his murderous work is done, rides back into the same mysterious nothingness, and there's a cut to his tombstone.

But in between the apocalyptic moments of creation and dissolution the landscape sends a multitude of other messages, messages that seem as true and incontrovertible as the mountains and plains. It is the genius of the Western that it seems to make the land speak for itself. So that when we read the line from Louis L'Amour's *Heller with a Gun*—"it was a hard land, and it bred hard men to hard ways"—we forget that this truth, so transparently self-evident, was propounded by a man sitting at a typewriter.

The land revealed on the opening pages or in the opening shot of a Western is a land defined by absence: of trees, of greenery, of houses, of the signs of civilization, above all, absence of water and shade. This description, from L'Amour's *Hondo*, is typical:

> It was hot. A few lost, cotton-ball bunches of cloud drifted in a brassy sky, leaving rare islands of shadow upon the desert's face.
>
> Nothing moved. It was a far, lost land, a land of beige-gray silences and distance where the eye reached out farther and farther to lose itself finally against the sky, and where the only movement was the lazy swing of a remote buzzard. (2)

It is an environment inimical to human beings, where a person is exposed, the sun beats down, and there is no place to hide. But the negations of the physical setting—no shelter, no water, no rest, no comfort—are also its siren song. Be brave, be strong enough to endure this, it says, and you will become like this—hard, austere, sublime. This code of asceticism founds our experience of Western stories. The landscape challenges the body to endure hardship—that is its fundamental message at the physical level. It says, This is a hard place to be; you will have to do without here. Its spiritual message is the same: come, and suffer.

The appeal of the desert lies partly in its promise of pain, an invitation that is irresistible, as Charles Sheldon suggested, because it awakens a desire for spiritual prowess, some unearthly glory earned through long-continued discipline, self-sacrifice, submission to a supernal power. Men may dominate or simply ignore women in Westerns, they may break horses and drive cattle, kill game and kick dogs and beat one another into a pulp, but they never lord it over nature. Nature is the one transcendent thing, the one thing larger than man (and it is constantly portrayed as immense), the ideal toward which human nature strives. Not *imitatio Christi* but *imitatio naturae*. What is imitated is a physical thing, not a spiritual ideal; a solid state of being, not a process of becoming; a material entity, not a person; a condition of objecthood, not a form of consciousness. The landscape's final invitation—merger—promises complete materialization. Meanwhile, the qualities that nature implicitly possesses—power, endurance, rugged majesty—are the ones that men desire while they live.

And so men imitate the land in Westerns; they try to look as much like nature as possible. Everything blends imperceptibly into the desert.

> He wore nothing that gleamed. The lineback's dun color shaded into the desert as did his own clothing.

> [His face] had all the characteristics of the range rider's—the leanness, the red burn of the sun, the set changelessness that came from years of silence and solitude.

> He was a big man, wide-shouldered, with the lean hardboned face of the desert rider. There was no softness in him. His toughness was ingrained and deep.

> He had plainly come many miles from somewhere across the vast horizon, as the dust upon him showed. His boots were white with it. His overalls were gray with it. The weather-beaten bloom of his face shone through it duskily.

These quotations, from *Hondo, Riders of the Purple Sage, Hondo*, and *The Virginian*, respectively, all describe the same man, a man whose hardness is one with the hardness of nature. L'Amour writes in the foreword to *Hondo* that his hero was a man "bleak as the land over which he rode." The cover of *Heller with a Gun* reads: "He was as merciless as the frontier that bred him." The qualities needed to survive on the land are the qualities the land itself possesses—bleakness, mercilessness. And they are regarded not only as necessary to survival but as the acme of human moral perfection. To be a man in the Western is to seem to grow out of the environment, which means to be hard, to be tough, to be unforgiving. The ethical system the Western proposes, which vindicates conflict, violence, and vengeance, and the social and political hierarchy it creates, putting adult white males on top with everyone else in descending order beneath—this code and this hierarchy never appear to reflect the interests or beliefs of any particular group, or of human beings at all, but seem to have been dictated primordially by nature itself.

For the setting by its hardness and austerity seems to have selected its heroes from among strong men in the prime of life, people who have a certain build, complexion, facial type, carriage, gesture, and demeanor; who dress a certain way, carry certain accoutrements, have few or no social ties, are expert at certain skills (riding, tracking, roping, fistfighting, shooting) and terrible at others (dancing, talking to ladies). And because the people who exhibit these traits in Westerns are invariably white, male, and Anglo-Saxon, the Western naturalizes a certain racial, gender, and ethnic type as hero. There is no need to *say* that men are superior to women, Anglos to Mexicans, white men to black; the scene has already said it.

Nature makes it obvious, even to the most benighted, who her chosen are; the sage-dotted plains, the buttes, the infinite sky tell more plainly than any words what is necessary in a man. The landscape establishes by contrast an image of the corrupt, effete life that the genre never tires of criticizing—the fancy words and pretty actions of the drawing room, elegant clothes, foreign accents, dusky complexions, subservient manners, of women, Easterners, and non-white males. We know that the people who get off the stage wearing suits and carrying valises, sporting parasols or mustaches, are doomed, not because of anything anyone says about them but because of the mountains in the background and the desert underfoot which is continuous with the main street of town. The female, the dusky, and the dressed up are not harsh and hard and pure like the desert. Not strong and silent and unforgiving. The harshness of the Western landscape is so rhetorically persuasive that an entire code of values is in place, rock solid, from the outset, without anyone's ever saying a word.

So the desert is the classic Western landscape, rather than the rain forests of the Pacific Northwest or the valleys of California, because of the messages it sends. It does not give of bird or bush. Fertility, abundance, softness, fluidity, many-layeredness are at a discount here. The desert offers itself as the white sheet on which to trace a figure. It is a tabula rasa on which man can write, as if for the first time, the story he wants to live. That is why the first moment of Western movies is so full of promise. It is the New World, represented here, not for the first time, as a void, the *vacuum domicilium* the Puritans had imagined, waiting to be peopled. The apparent emptiness makes the land desirable not only as a space to be filled but also as a stage on which to perform and as a territory to master.

When a man walks or rides into a forest, he is lost among the trees, can't see ahead, doesn't know what might be lurking there. The forest surrounds him, obscures him with shadows, confuses itself with him by its vertical composition and competitive detail. But when a lone horseman appears on the desert plain, he dominates it instantly, his view extends as far as the eye can see, and enemies are exposed to his gaze. The desert flatters the human figure by making it seem dominant and unique, dark against light, vertical against horizontal, solid against plane, detail against blankness. And the openness of the space means that domination can take place virtually through the act of opening one's eyes, through the act, even, of watching a representation on a screen. The openness also

Still from *McKenna's Gold* (Columbia, 1969).
Courtesy of the Museum of Modern Art/Film Stills Archive, New York.

provides infinite access. There is nothing to stop the horseman's free movement across the terrain. He can conquer it by traversing it, know it by standing on it. Distance, made palpable through exposure and infinitely prolonged by the absence of obstacles, offers unlimited room to move. The man can go, in any direction, as far as he can go. The possibilities are infinite.

The blankness of the plain implies—without ever stating—that this is a field where a certain kind of mastery is possible, where a person (of a certain kind) can remain alone and complete and in control of himself, while controlling the external world through physical strength and force of will. The Western situates itself characteristically in the desert because the desert seems by its very existence to affirm that life must be seen from the point of view of death, that physical stamina and strength are the sine qua non of personal distinction, that matter and physical force are the substance of ultimate reality, and that sensory experience, the history of the body's contact with things, is the repository of all significant knowledge. It chooses the desert because its clean, spare lines, lucid spaces, and absence of ornament bring it closer to the abstract austerities of modern architectural design than any other kind of landscape would. The Western deifies nature—the nonhuman—and yet the form of nature it chooses for the site of its worship is the one most resembling man-made space: monumental.

This architectural quality is not an accident but is integral to the way the landscape functions psychologically in Westerns. It expresses a need to be in control of one's surroundings, to dominate them; hence the denuded, absolute quality of the scene which recalls the empty canyons of city streets, blank, mute, and hostile to human purposes. At the same time the monolithic, awe-inspiring character of the landscape seems to reflect a desire for self-transcendence, an urge to join the self to something greater. In representing space that is superhuman but man-made, domineering and domineered, the Western both glorifies nature *and* suppresses it simultaneously.

Power, more than any other quality, is what is being celebrated and struggled with in these grandiose vistas. The worship of power, the desire for it, and, at the same time, an awe of it bordering on reverence and dread emanate from these panoramic, wide-angle views. There is a romance going on here. The landscape arouses the viewer's desire for, wish to identify with, an object that is overpowering and majestic, an object that draws the viewer ineluctably to itself and crushes him with the thought of its greatness and ineffability.

This, at least, is the rhetoric of the landscape Westerns revel in. It is, of course, an interpretation of nature that produces the impressions I have been describing. The various kinds of hardness nature seems to inculcate in Western novels and films are projected onto the landscape by men and read back off it by them—images of the heart's desires and fears. For the desert is no more blank or empty than the northeastern forests were when the Europeans came. It is full of living things, of birds and animals, and inhabited by people. When you first come to the desert, writes John C. Van Dyke (one of the great Anglo chroniclers of the American desert, writing for others of a similar background),

> you see little more than a desolate waste. . . . The vegetation you think looks like a thin covering of dry sticks. And as for the animals, the birds—the living things on the desert—they are not apparent at all. . . . Yet they are here. Even in the lava-beds where not even cactus will grow, and where to all appearance there is no life whatever, you may see tracks in the sand where quail and road-runners and linnets have been running about in search of food. There are tracks, too, of the coyote and the wild-cat—tracks following tracks. . . . (174–75)

The emptiness we see in the desert, the sense of a hostile environment, is an effect of a certain way of life and of certain desires. Western "nature" exists not in itself but through and for Eastern men's eyes.

The rhetoric of the landscape works in favor of the particular masculine ideal Westerns enforce. But it is only in the split second at the beginning, say, of *Gunfight at the OK Corral* when all you see is the line of the horizon, perfectly flat and unbroken, that the landscape really possesses the monolithic austerity I have been ascribing to it. As soon as the tiny figures of the horsemen appear, or a wagon or a wagon train, as soon as the line is broken even by sage brush or cattle or mountains, the signs of life undo the still perfection of objecthood. In fact, the land is almost never truly blank but is wrinkled and folded and written on in a variety of ways. One of the hero's chief skills is his ability to decipher it. L'Amour's heroes are constantly pausing to read "sign," the telltale traces of animals and men, or the signals that nature leaves lying around to point those who know in the direction of what they're looking for—water, pasture, game, a place to camp for the night.

Not only is the landscape almost never truly blank, but it is constantly changing, continually inviting the senses, stimulating feeling, perception, and thought. At any particular moment, the landscape wears an individual face with distinguishing features, which Western writers never tire of describing. They are always telling you how the sage smelled and how fast the clouds were moving and what shape the shadows had along the edge of the ravine. L'Amour in particular is captivated by the rich potential of the terrain his characters move across; the single most important relationship they have is to the land. They are in constant contact with it—thinking about it, using it, enjoying it, fearing it, seeing it, smelling it, touching it, hearing it. The rhythms of the landscape's appearance and disappearance in the hero's consciousness, the way it impinges on his mind, body, and emotions, are fundamental to the experience Western narratives provide. Feel, for example, the sensations of this passage from L'Amour's *Sackett* (1961):

> We started up Coyote Creek in the late hours of the night, with stars hanging their bright lanterns over the mountains. Cap was riding point, our six pack horses trailing him, and me riding drag. A chill wind came down off the Sangre de Cristos, and somewhere out over the bottom a quail was calling.
>
> Cap had a sour, dry-mouthed look to him. He was the kind if you got in trouble you didn't look to see if he was still with you—you knew damned well he was.
>
> Not wishing to be seen leaving, we avoided Mora, and unless somebody was lying atop that rocky ridge near the ranch it was unlikely that we were seen.
>
> The Mora river flowed through a narrow gap at the ranch and out into the flatlands beyond, and we had only to follow the Mora until it was joined by Coyote Creek, then turned up Coyote and across the wide valley of La Cueva.
>
> We circled around the sleeping village of Golondrinos, and pointed

north, shivering in the morning cold. The sky was stark and clear, the ridges sharply cut against the faintly lightening sky. Grass swished about our horses' hoofs, our saddles creaked, and over at Golondrinos a dog barked inquiringly into the morning. (37–38)

Passages like this, with their continual scoping of the landscape, are the staple of Western fiction, its bread of life. The body of the land provides a field of action and a fund of sensation, and the place names (Golondrinos, Coyote Creek, Sangre de Cristos) lend historicity and romance. In this excerpt the narrator is distanced from his surroundings, relatively speaking; physical sensations are enough to situate the reader but not intense, the quail calling "somewhere out over the bottom" providing just a touch of specificity. The paragraph about Cap interrupts the geographical focus momentarily, and then the narrator's movements are recounted in summary fashion: "we avoided Mora," "turned up Coyote," "circled around the sleeping village." Still, spatial location, the lay of the land, and the body's sensations in the environment dominate, and the passage concludes characteristically in a moment of heightened awareness: a shiver in the cold, sharply outlined ridges, swishing grass, creaking saddle leather, and a dog that "barked inquiringly into the morning." The moment consists not in thought or emotion, not in action or reaction, but in the textural features of the landscape, tallied and imprinted on the senses. To feel that moment, through and through, is what people turn to Westerns for.

Later, when the hero is on the trail of someone he is searching for, the focus zooms in close:

I walked my horse across a high meadow that lay beyond the curtain of trees. The ground was nigh covered by alpine gold-flower, bright yellow, and almighty pretty to look at. And along some of the trickles running down from the melting snow a kind of primrose was growing.

The trees were mostly blue spruce, shading off into aspen and, on the high ridges above timberline, there were a few squat bristle-cone pines, gnarled from their endless war with the wind.

A couple of times I found where whoever it was I was trailing had

stopped to pick some kind of herb out of the grass, or to drink at a
stream. (64–65)

This conscientious registry of the terrain, which occupies six solid
pages at this point in the text, is not at all unusual. The hero moves
over the land with an intensity of concentration that turns his journey into a drama of exploration. He rides through forests and into
meadows, across ridges and down canyons, scales mountainsides,
follows streams, pausing constantly to study the land and plot his
next move. The scenery changes dramatically.

> The boulders were a maze. Great slabs of rock stood on knife edges,
> looking like rows of broken molars, split and rotten. Without warning
> a canyon dropped away in front of me for maybe five hundred feet of
> almost sheer fall. Off to the left I could see an eyebrow of trail. (67)

With the mention of human features, eyebrow and teeth, L'Amour
hints at the personhood that lurks beneath the landscape's surface.
The hero and the landscape perform a pas de deux; he rides, walks,
crawls, climbs across it, stops to touch, smell, listen, and scrutinize,
while the land responds with an ever-changing series of vistas, challenges, clues, surprises, mysteries. Characteristically, as I've said,
the landscape is the site of ordeal, proving the man as nothing else
can—in *Sackett*, for instance, shortly after the passage just cited,
the hero climbs the talus of a hill and then works his way up a rock
chimney until he stands two thousand feet above the valley floor,
as a sort of warm-up exercise. But the land doesn't just test men; it
also rewards them with food, water, shelter, and, finally, rest. This
passage from L'Amour's *Silver Canyon* (1956) is typical:

> Behind me the Sweet Alice Hills lifted their rough shoulders, all of a
> thousand feet higher than the spring where I was camped. . . . The sun
> was setting over the Blue Mountains and, hunkered down over a tiny
> fire, I prepared my supper, worried and on edge because of all that
> might be happening.
>
>   Yet, as the evening drew on, my anxiety left me. The hills were silent
> and dark. There was only a faint trickling of water from the spring, and
> the comfortable, quieting sound of my horse cropping grass. (116)

The hero's passage across the landscape has ultimately a domesticating effect. Though it begins in anxious movement and passes through terror and pain, it continually ends in repose. A welcoming grove of aspens, a spring, and a patch of grass provide shelter and sustenance. A campfire and the setting sun give visual pleasure and comfort, while trickling water and a horse cropping grass make soothing noises. If nature's wildness and hardness test his strength and will and intelligence, they also give him solace and refreshment.

Perhaps more than anything, nature gives the hero a sense of himself. For he is competent in this setting. He knows his horse will lead him to water, knows how to build a fire and where to camp. He can take care of himself. Besides being agonistic and at times ecstatic, the hero's relationship to the environment is steady, knowledgeable, functional, and pleasure-giving. Over and over, as he feeds and waters his horse, builds a fire, cooks his supper, and beds down for the night, he makes the world answer his primary needs. There is something infinitely reassuring about this. Far from town, far from the conveniences of modern life, far from any outside help, the solitary man, with only nature at his disposal, makes himself comfortable. He does so in answer, perhaps, to the reader's wish that the universe turn out, finally, to be a safe place for him also, not a mine field or a prison but a maternal home.

The interaction between hero and landscape lies at the genre's center, overshadowed in the popular image of the Western by gunfights and chases, but no less essential to the experience Westerns provide. In the end, the land is everything to the hero; it is both the destination and the way. He courts it, struggles with it, defies it, conquers it, and lies down with it at night. In this, it is like nothing so much as the figure the Western casts out at the start: the woman. If the hero wants to become a phallic butte, immovable and sere, imitating the "great slabs of rock" that "stood on knife edges," he also wants to embrace the ground he walks on, "the high meadow . . . behind a curtain of trees, covered with gold alpine flower," with "trickles running down from melting snow."

The alternation of challenging vistas of desert and rock that demand competition and struggle with inviting pastoral interludes offering pleasure and nurturance turns the landscape into a kind of gender allegory where the land plays a series of roles. In the passage from *Silver Canyon* the hero has started out from Poison Canyon and passed through Dark Canyon, but he ends up in sight of the Sweet Alice Hills. In films, the staple setting of dry rock and scrub-dotted sand is punctuated by shots of flowing rivers bordered by green trees, as, for example, in *The Wild Bunch*, where the river shots are breathtakingly sensual and the desert sequences unbearably parched and sunstruck.

In the faithfully and minutely recorded passage of the hero's body over the body of the land, in his constant interaction with it, mental and physical, the hero plays out his social relationships, answers his spiritual needs, and foreshadows his destiny. So much so that it is tempting to say the hero's relation to the land is a substitute relation. No sex in the Western? No women? No home? Get yourself to the Sweet Alice Hills, or better yet the Grand Tetons (French for "big breasts"), and find relief.

Yet while it is probably true in some sense that the land takes the place of things the Western does not and will not represent, the trouble with this view is that it limits the possible meanings of the genre to a narrow and highly conventional range of alternatives. To say that the hero's palpation of the land really takes the place of sex with a woman, that his bedding down and making himself comfortable in it really substitutes for the domestic fireside and a mother's care, or that his struggle to survive it reenacts his competition with other men assumes that heterosexual sexuality, the nuclear family, and a struggle for status among peers are the bedrock of all human experience. My sense is that these are precisely the structures of experience that the landscape in Westerns is trying to displace. The man who leaves home and fireside and turns to the wilderness does so in search of something other than what they have to offer.

In looking for a way to express the something other that the landscape represents, I came upon a book that describes a turn to the desert that took place fifteen hundred years ago in the Middle East. Benedicta Ward's *The Desert Christian* (1975), which describes the founding of Christian monasticism, may seem distant from the West of John Wayne and Clint Eastwood, but it provides a suggestive parallel for a similar turn to the desert that took place in the twentieth-century imagination.

St. Anthony the Great, the hermit of Lower Egypt, Ward says in her foreword, gave all he had to the poor, devoted himself to asceticism under the guidance of a recluse for several years, and at age thirty-four went into the desert to live in complete solitude for the rest of his life. In Upper Egypt, communities of brothers living in the desert, united to one another in work and prayer, formed the basis for later organized monasticism. In Nitria and Scetis, desert monks lived together under the direction of a spiritual father, or "abba." And in Syria monks "deliberately imposed on themselves what is hardest for human beings to bear: they went about naked and in chains, they lived unsettled lives, eating whatever they found in the woods, . . . [choosing] to live at the limits of human nature, close to the animals, the angels, and the demons." These events took place around the year A.D. 400.

For the desert Christians, the first step in this life was withdrawal from ordinary society. The second was placing themselves under a spiritual father. After that, the rule was living as simply as possible. "One hour's sleep a night is enough for a monk if he is a fighter." "For a man of prayer, one meal a day is sufficient." No possessions besides a hut, a reed mat, a sheep skin, a lamp, and a vessel for water or oil. There was not much talking, economy of words being as important as economy of things. The desert fathers gave life to their disciples through the word, used sparingly and conceived as part of a relationship. Most of the sayings of the fathers concern the best way to live in the body and the day-to-day struggle with the passions (especially sexual passion). "It was this aspect of warfare with the demons that was called 'ascesis,' the hard work of being a monk." Its aim was *hesychia*, "quiet, the calm through the whole man" (xxiv).

I detail these practices to suggest the parallels between desert monasticism and the features that define the Western hero's existence. Not that Westerns derive historically from desert monasticism, or that their belief system reflects that of the desert fathers. Rather, the similarities point to a dimension of the Western's ethos that otherwise might be missed.

Westerns give small rein to the body's need for food, sleep, shelter, sex, and overall comfort. The cowboy's fare—on the few occasions that he eats—is hardtack, boiled coffee, and cigarettes. Sometimes just the cigarette. Thirst is constant, sleep characteristically denied. The hero makes camp for a few short hours and then, while the stars are still out, saddles up and is on his way. ("For Hondo," writes L'Amour, "to wake was to rise.") The capacity to stand physical pain, as I've suggested, is central to the hero's identity.

The hero almost never has sex, and when he does it's only implied, not shown, denial of sex being central to the kind of deprivation the Western finds essential for the exemplary life. Like the absence of greenery, it is a turning away from fertility, fluidity, propagation, and an affirmation of what is hard and dry and takes a long time to come to fruition. For the desert itself is the great exemplar of ascesis. The hero imitates the desert's fierceness in his hard struggle to survive, its loneliness in his solitary existence, and its silence in his frugal way with language. Gnomic, carved out of life experience, compressed and delivered under pressure, the sayings of cowboy heroes, by their brevity, acknowledge, as do the saying of the desert fathers, the importance of things that cannot be said.

And here lies another paradox: the desert landscape is the fullest realization of the genre's drive toward materiality, the place where language fails and rocks assert themselves. But by the same token it is the place where something else becomes visible, an ineffable thing that cannot be named. The desert pushes the consciousness of the hero and of the reader/viewer beyond itself and into another realm. The buttes are still, the mountains remain unmoved, the sun beats down, the horizon recedes forever beneath the sky. It is not only the body that is tested here; the desert is a spiritual proving ground as well. The landscape, which on the one hand drives Christianity away, ends by forcing men to see something godlike there. "All I know," says a character from L'Amour's *The Lonesome Gods* (1983), "is that I shall never rest easy until I have gone into the desert alone."

TOWN

In certain Westerns, both novels and films, I feel a tremendous desire to be in town, the town the hero rides into somewhere near the beginning of the story. The way the lights and shadows fall across the wooden sidewalks and onto the sides of the buildings—the dry goods store, the law office, the newspaper office—the scurrying children, women in their long dresses and bonnets and shawls, horses tied to the hitching rail, the water trough, the sound of the blacksmith's hammer, the dust from wagons going by, the leather harnesses, the iron wheels—everything about this scene arouses a craving in me to travel back in time to that place and live the life that is implied in these details. It is home, safe, authentic, the way life was meant to be—close to the earth, to the land, to the senses, to good materials, to sun and wind and dust, to people and animals. This town represents a simpler, more benign social order, a place for everyone and everyone in her place.

There is a tremendous tension in Westerns between the landscape and town. The genre pulls toward the landscape—that, in a sense, is its whole point. But because there's so much emphasis on getting away, town also exerts a tremendous pull; otherwise there would be no reason to flee. So there's a paradox in the presentation of town.

Town is a mecca, a haven, journey's end. The men go there to get supplies, to eat, to sleep, to rest up from their labors—ranching, mining, chasing bandits, hiding out, fighting each other. They come to town for respite and refuge. To get a shave, a haircut, a bath, to put on clean clothes and feel human again. They come to get drunk and play cards and ogle the saloon girls. They come to wheel and deal and steal and get information. They come to meet the train or the stage. Town is a magnet; it draws people. Or a well, a place people come to to draw something out, some form of sustenance; it holds the bank that characters in Westerns are always robbing.

So town functions as a surrogate home, though it's not home because it's a public place. It supplies things that humans need—physical comforts, companionship—yet it does this largely without imposing the obligations the hero is in retreat from. (That is the purpose of the saloon, the place where food and drink and sex can all be bought.) But in fact, town always threatens to entrap the hero in the very things the genre most wishes to avoid: intimacy, mutual dependence, a network of social and emotional responsibilities. Town fills basic needs, but basic though they are, they are precisely the needs that have to be denied because of what their satisfaction inevitably entails. Town seduces.

When the hero enters the saloon after being out in the desert, all the senses are eased—the desire for shade, coolness, something to drink, a place to sit down, human companionship. In the background, the saloon girl's breasts, her dress, her hair, her voice if she is singing, her red lips, all a reminder of what the cowboy has for so long done without, and must continue to renounce if he is to survive.

Now pull the camera gradually away from the smoky card table, back through the swinging doors of the saloon. Dolly back down Main Street; let the false fronts show their shrunken hind parts; let the buildings grow smaller, until finally they are a tiny silhouette against a range of desert mountains rising up behind. Now let the sky dwarf everything, until town is nothing but a squidge on a vast plain, mountain-rimmed and arched by an even vaster heaven. Here, in plain and sky and mountain, is what *is*, what the horseman rides out of and back into, the beginning and the end.

The Western is always bombinating between these alternatives: town, where if a bullet doesn't get you a woman will, and desert, where death waits in a different form. For there is often a link, at the final moment of Westerns, between the desert and the town. They seem to be opposed, and for the most part they are, but in this moment a rapprochement occurs. When the hero meets his enemy face to face, someone dies and someone rides away, but both bodies bend toward the land—one prone or supine, in the dust, and one upright and mounted, on its way. On its way across a dusty plain that reminds us of a fate postponed.

"In Without Knocking," by Charles M. Russell, 1909. (Oil on canvas).
Courtesy of the Amon Carter Museum, Fort Worth, Texas (accession no. 1961.201).

Horses

4

'A fiery horse with the speed of light, a cloud of dust and a hearty hi-ho Silver! The Lone Ranger!" These words, declaimed to the sound of the *William Tell* Overture, accompany the opening shot of "The Lone Ranger"—a close-up of a big white horse, ridden at a gallop by a masked rider. As the words "THE LONE RANGER" cover the image, we hear *bang, bang*. The camera pulls back. The Lone Ranger and Silver gallop down into a sage-dotted valley, draw up momentarily in front of a butte, wheel, then take off again, Silver's white mane and tail waving in the wind.

Now, try to imagine the same sequence without the horse . . .

Just as in "The Lone Ranger" there are certain things you take for granted, so it is in Westerns generally. You expect the sage-dotted plains, the buttes, the town with its false fronts, sandy main street, saloon, livery stable, cowboys in jeans and ten gallon hats. And horses: in town tied to the hitching rail, being ridden by a single rider outlined against the sky, pulling wobbly covered wagons, free on the prairie. In the background, in the foreground, on the margins, at the center, horses are on the screen constantly, seen in every conceivable attitude. The presence of such beings has an extraordinary influence on our experience of Westerns. The sheer energy of the posse, chasing the bandits at breakneck speed, pulling up short, the horses' mouths foaming, bridles clanking, saddles creaking, hooves churning the sand; the fleeing villains stopping at a lookout point, wheeling around, pausing for a moment, then turning and galloping off again in a cloud of dust—these images are the heart and soul of a Western.

But though horses in Westerns are de rigueur, the characters who ride them don't pay them much attention, and as far as the critics are concerned they might as well not exist. The index to one of the most complete treatments of a corpus of Westerns ever written— Tag Gallagher's excellent *John Ford: The Man and His Films*— lists in boldface heroes, Indians, homosexuality, home, innocence, wilderness, rivers, good badmen, drunks, determinism, and destiny, but it doesn't list horses, although Ford, who made more than sixty Westerns, was almost unique in recognizing their importance; that is, he seemed to really *see* horses in a way other directors didn't. Horses, in Westerns, are precisely what meets the eye; that is, physically, visually, they are right there in front of you, but no one seems to notice them in the sense of paying them any attention. Because of this strange invisibility they are the place where everything in the genre is hidden. Besides doing all the work in a literal sense, getting the characters from place to place, pulling wagons, plowing fields, and such, they do double, triple, quadruple work in a symbolic sense. The more you look at them, the more indispensable they seem.

Ford's favorite movie, *Wagonmaster*, is an excellent place to begin looking at horses in Westerns, since it is the only Western film I know that registers consciously the lack of fit between the way characters in Westerns treat horses and the salient, dynamic presence of the animals themselves. The movie starts with a panorama full of horses and wagon wheels and dogs and men, shot against a backdrop of sheltering mountains. This long overture expressing the sweep of history and the grandeur of nature suggests that the story about to unfold should be seen in an epic context. In the first scene,

two good-natured horse traders named Sandy and Travis, surrounded by horses, talk about them purely as income producers.
"The way I figure, Travis, these ponies are going to bring us thirty
dollars a head." Coming after the panoramic overture, this seems
a comically reductive way to talk. We get the impression of men
who are part of something much larger than they are—the settling
of the West, the ongoing life of nature—of which they haven't the
remotest conception.

In the next scene Travis sells a horse to the town marshal, describing him in a formulaic singsong way—"sound and strong, eye,
wind and limb"—that seems to have nothing to do with the horse
we actually see. In the following scene, where the supposedly gentle
horse lands the marshal in the dust, the horse's bravura performance
is ironically juxtaposed to the counting out of money. Again, the
human characters seem to have tunnel vision. The bucking bronco
is only money to them, a clever bargain ("eight, nine, ten"), but
the camera sees it as animal energy, an unquenchable life force
fighting back.

In the last scene in the sequence, some Mormons who have
just arrived in town offer to buy Travis and Sandy's horses at the
asking price—fifty dollars a head—with an extra hundred thrown
in if they'll lead the Mormon wagon train to the San Juan Valley. The entire negotiation takes place in front of a corral fence,
behind which the remuda of horses moves restlessly. Though a
liminal element only, the horses seem more strongly present
than ever. In the glimpses we catch of them milling around tu-
multuously, their piercing whinnies breaking into the conversation, in the tossing of a mane and the flash of an eye, their dust
and commotion, they exert pressure on the foregrounded action,
interrupting it, energizing it, surrounding it in a way that doesn't
force us to note them consciously but affects our senses constantly as we watch the scene. Ford uses this technique throughout the movie. Later on, when Travis proposes marriage to a

woman while they walk along next to his horse, the screen is divided into three parts: the horse's head, Travis, and the woman. While the horse is silent, he is *socially* present throughout, an active listener and participant in the action.

The ironic distance Ford opens up between horses as he makes us see them, and horses as the characters see them, replicates the irony of the title *Wagonmaster*. Travis, it turns out, doesn't really know the way to the San Juan Valley, and the movie makes it clear how little he, or any single person, has mastery over wagons, horses, rivers, people, or anything. Horses, in fact, not only come to symbolize the epic scope of the enterprise, they also begin to stand for something larger even than the historical movement the film commemorates. Midway through the story, as the Mormons are making their way across another river, and one wagon's team is being urged up the farther bank by a mounted horseman, a foal appears running free ahead of the horses in harness, up the bank and out of sight into the trees. The same footage appears as the closing shot of the movie, transforming the sense of finality conveyed by the Mormons' arrival in the San Juan Valley into a sense of continuing process. The foal, running on ahead of the rest and disappearing off the screen, is ongoing life, pressing forward into the future, innocent and free, free from wagons, free from masters, free from the movie itself.

The paradox of horses in Western movies is this: you can't have a Western without them, visually they are everywhere, and symbolically they carry a tremendous payload, but the mind doesn't count them in its inventory or give them any more of the time of day than the characters in *Wagonmaster* do. When we look at a picture on the screen consisting of men and horses, we never think about whether the horses are tired, or want to be galloping after the villains, or, if asked, would choose to pull covered wagons across the plains. When we look at the picture, though horses may affect our reactions subliminally, on a conscious level we think only about the men.

So the question is, What are horses *doing* in Westerns? Their presence seems natural to us, but for most of the nineteenth century horses figured very little in popular fiction. Their gradual appearance, first in dime novels, then in major best-sellers and in films at the beginning of the twentieth century coincides with the disappearance of horses from daily life, where they were used as work animals and as a means of transportation. This suggests that horses fulfill a longing for a different *kind* of existence. Antimodern, antiurban, and antitechnological, they stand for an existence without cars and telephones and electricity. But you could have narratives set on farms or in small towns that embraced the simple life without filling them full of horses. Why horses in particular? And why only in certain forms? It isn't the farm horse primarily that we associate with Westerns, or the horse as show animal; it is horses ridden by men, charging into town, charging out of town, outlined on high mesas looking into the distance, coming at you at a gallop pulling a fleeing stagecoach, riding herd on the dogies as they move into the draw, or running free and wild.

Horses reach back to something in the past, in the 1870s, '80s, and '90s after the Civil War. But what they reach back for is not just some generalized notion of rural existence. Horses are something people have close physical contact with, something they touch, press against with their bodies. Something that is alive, first of all, something big, powerful, and fast-moving. Something not human but not beyond human control, dangerous, even potentially lethal, but ductile to the human will.

The key to what horses represent in Westerns is something very simple. It is the fact that the body of the horse stands beneath the body of the rider, between the human being and the earth. Horses express a need for connection to nature, to the wild. But it is nature in a particular form. Not songbirds or running brooks or violets by mossy stones, but power, motion, size, strength, brought under human control and in touch with the human body. It is the physical existence of horses above all that makes them indispensable in West-

erns. Their dynamic material presence, their energy and corporeality
call out to the bodies of the viewers, to our bodies. Film after film
begins with the tiny figures of horsemen outlined against the horizon, growing larger as they move nearer the camera, until finally
you can hear their hoofbeats, see the whites of their eyes, be excited
by their mass and motion. Right up to the camera they come so
we can vicariously be in contact with their flesh, feel their breath,
sense their strength and stamina, absorb the flow of force. Horses
are there to galvanize us. More than any other single element in
the genre, they symbolize the desire to recuperate some lost connection to life.

This connection can be dangerous. Of all Western writers, Zane
Grey felt the apocalyptic possibilities of nature most profoundly.
He captures the perilous, ecstatic, and godlike eruptions of natural force in spectacular prose. What men cannot do in Grey,
horses and landscape will; the boundaries between his characters
and their surroundings—animal, vegetable, and mineral—continually break down, and everything becomes part of a vortex of
live energy coursing indiscriminately through the cosmos. At the
end of a novel about horses called *Wildfire*, the hero rides a
horse named Wildfire through a forest fire that has gone out of
control. He is trying to save the girl he loves, who is strapped
naked to the back of another horse. The wildfire, "freed from the
bowels of the earth, tremendous, devouring," is the analogue of
the hero's own passion. "The intense and abnormal rider's passion . . . dammed up, but never fully controlled, burst within him,
and suddenly he awoke to a wild and terrible violence of heart and
soul. He had accepted death; he had no fear. All that he wanted
to do, the last thing he wanted to do, was to ride down the King
and kill Lucy mercifully." In this climactic scene, where everything
is heated to the melting point, the hero lusts to kill what he loves.

Love and murder are intermingled and confused, just as the forest fire (wildfire) and the horse (Wildfire) and human passion (wildfire) have blended indistinguishably.

The energy horses represent is destructive and creative. Though in *Wildfire* both horses and human beings survive the cataclysmic eruption, in other incidents in Grey's work, such as the great "Wrangle's Race Run" chapter of *Riders of the Purple Sage*, the climatic ride of a heroic horse ends in death. It's not surprising that in most Westerns the perilous, sexually charged, rapturous potentiality of horses which Grey so well understood is kept in abeyance. Too apocalyptic, too threatening to our everyday categories of being and becoming, the volcanic force is typically rationed and controlled—in chase scenes, in episodes of horse breaking, and in occasional glimpses of bands of wild horses running free. Most of the time, the Western prefers its horses in manageable form, the most manageable being that exemplified in the opening of "The Guns of Will Sonnett," a fifties serial still shown sometimes on late-night TV.

It begins with an old man and a young boy ambling along on their horses. It's a sunny day, the sky is blue, the hills are a warm brown, and these two—four, really, because the horses are just as much a part of the scene as the men are—are just taking their time. The easygoing reciprocity between them, communicated not through language but through relaxed and rhythmical movements as horse and rider amble comfortably along, epitomizes, from a human point of view, the right relation of creatures to one another. The relation the man and horse embody is echoed in the sociableness and tacit trust between the friends (in this case grandfather and grandson), a relationship of mutual regard, mutual knowledge, and mutual acceptance. The Will Sonnett opener represents the ideal version of the horse-human relation (from the human point of view): men, animals, and landscape constituting a sort of peaceable kingdom.

In *Monte Walsh* (1970), a film starring Lee Marvin and Jack Palance, the horse takes over the role of human companionship altogether in a closing scene that wittily echoes the beginning of the story. At the opening, the hero and his pal come across a wolf on the prairie, and the following dialogue ensues:

MONTE WALSH (*referring to the wolf-pelt*) How nice, another five dollars. Did I ever tell you about Big Joe Amati?

PAL No.

MONTE Well, he used to wrestle wolves. Well, I never seen him do it, but I heard tell and I always wondered how you would wrestle a wolf.

PAL What you waitin' for?

MONTE I wonder how you *would* wrestle a wolf.

PAL Jesus. (*He takes his gun and shoots the wolf.*)

In the film's closing scene, after the hero has lost his lover and his pal, he is riding across the prairie by himself and comes upon a wolf. He dismounts, and the following dialogue ensues:

MONTE Did I ever tell you about Big Joe Amati? (*Horse looks around.*)

HORSE Neigh.

MONTE Well, he used to wrestle these. Well, I never seen him do it but I heard tell, and I know I . . . (*Horse looks around.*)

MONTE I always wondered how you would wrestle a wolf.

HORSE Neigh.

MONTE Well, we got better things to do than shoot wolves. (*Walks off, leading his horse into the brush.*) Now, let me tell you about Big Joe Amati. This boy was big. Now he come up around Denver way. . . .

Cut. End of film.

Monte Walsh's horse winds up taking the place of friend and lover, a situation the character accepts with wry humor and a certain self-satisfied resignation. As helpmeet and companion, the horse evokes from the hero sociable and nurturing behavior, perhaps because he is a safe repository for it. It is here, in the society of man and horse, that the problems women and language pose for the Western hero come closest to being solved. Free from emotional entanglements, yet in touch with a sentient being, the hero can commune with the world and feel his kinship with it by means of a relationship that is steady, rewarding, and to a certain degree mutual. The horse as friend and helpmeet, a pal through thick and thin, fulfills a dream of companionship as deep as the longing for wild abandon that Zane Grey's horses answer.

The sense of comradery and peaceful coexistence between man and horse should, perhaps, modify our sense of the endings of many Westerns. When the hero has to leave town at the end of the story and gets back on his horse and rides into the desert, he is not unaccommodated. The saddle he sits on is large and comfortable, and usually ornamented; to it are appended all sorts of gear—canteens, rifles, ropes, knives, bags of food, blankets, articles of clothing. There is a homeyness about all this equipment, so neatly stowed. The saddle leather creaks companionably, the bridle and the spurs jingle. The clip-clop of the hooves beat out a pleasant rhythm. The horse is the hero's home on the range, a mobile home to be sure, but better than a real house or a real trailer because it is alive, someone to talk to, to count on when the going gets tough. When he leaves the girl at the end of the movie, the hero isn't going off into the wild blue yonder all by himself; he is coming home to his horse, and together they are going to seek new adventures.

Yet against all this, and at the same time bound up with it, runs another set toward horses in Western films. It is only after something has been done to them that horses become the benign substitutes for culture and society that Western films imagine. The desire to curb the horse and make it submit to human requirements is as important to Westerns as the desire for merger or mutuality. Horses do not start out as pals; they have to be forced into it.

Here are two stories Westerns tell about this process. In the first television episode of "The Lone Ranger," the Lone Ranger, left for dead by bandits who have killed all the other men in his party, is found by Tonto, who nurses him back to life in a cave with running water. It takes three days. After this, the Lone Ranger and Tonto are friends for life, Tonto promising, like the biblical Ruth, to go where the Lone Ranger goes. In the second episode, which mirrors the first remarkably, the hero sets out to find himself a horse. He directs Tonto to accompany him to Wild Horse Valley, where they find a beautiful white stallion wounded and lying on the ground, about to be gored to death by a buffalo. While Tonto shoots the buffalo, the Lone Ranger moves to the horse's side and decides he will try to save him. He and Tonto nurse him, as the voice-over says, "as best they can," and after a few days the horse seems better. "Can the wild stallion rise?" asks the voice-over. "Gently the masked man coaxes the horse." Soon the Lone Ranger and the horse become inseparable.

This scene of rescue mirrors still another, shown in flashback, in which the Lone Ranger, as a young man, had come upon an Indian boy, left to die by the marauders who had killed his family. He saves the boy, who would, of course, grow up to be Tonto and save his life in turn.

So the rescue of the white stallion has a long pedigree. The horse enters the story in the same way humans do. They all go through a process of death and rebirth that implies an equality among them, as well as relations of mutual nurturance and support. But just as the Lone Ranger and Tonto do not end up as equals, although each saves the other, so the horse and his rescuer are not equals either. When the stallion is on his feet and has cantered off a little distance, the Lone Ranger says, "I'd like that horse more than anything in the world. But if he wants to go, he should be free." The emphasis here falls on the hero's liberality: he will not possess the stallion against his will. But it also reveals the man's assumption that when a horse is owned by a man, the horse gives up his freedom.

The stallion, of course, *chooses* to do just that. As Tonto voluntarily becomes the Lone Ranger's servant (he doesn't use the word, of course), so the horse becomes his servant, too, though again the word is different. The Lone Ranger says, "We're going to be pals, aren't we, Silver?" But Silver figures chiefly as a means of transportation.

The contradiction between the Lone Ranger's actual relationship to Silver (master, owner, rider) and the only one that is acknowledged explicitly (pal) is striking. After the Lone Ranger puts a saddle on Silver, "and for the first time in his life, Silver bears weight on his back," there's a shot of the Lone Ranger riding around on Silver, and the voice-over declares portentously: "Here is no conflict between animal and master; here instead is a partnership between horse and rider. The Lone Ranger and Silver accept each other as equals."

The Lone Ranger's gentleness with Silver betokens a consideration that is real, just as real as the desire expressed in the voice-over's speech for reciprocity with horses, closeness, equality. But when a man is literally in the saddle and the other animal is underneath bearing the weight, that is not a relationship among equals. When one being holds the reins attached to a bit in the other being's mouth, when the rider wears spurs that are meant to gore the sides of the mount to urge him to go faster, when the rider gives the commands and the horse carries them out, when the rider *owns* the horse, that is not a relationship among equals. The piece of dialogue that brings the "finding of Silver" abruptly to a close unintentionally dramatizes what will become the standard position of horses in this serial, as in Westerns generally: they are a background condition.

LONE RANGER He's a beauty, Tonto, a dream horse if I ever
             rode one.
      TONTO Him and Scout good friends.

LONE RANGER Yes, they'll do a lot of riding side by side.
TONTO We ride after Cavendish gang now?

Like a dream house, a dream horse provides a setting for the
hero, an appropriate complement to his appearance. (Silver's white
coat and black saddle and bridle rhyme visually with the Lone
Ranger's black mask and white hat.) But once the horse is possessed,
most of the dream element disappears. With amazing rapidity, the
next dream takes its place. "We ride after Cavendish gang now?"
Tonto asks impatiently. And the Lone Ranger sets out to conquer
the Cavendish gang, forgetting all about Silver, although of course
he's riding on Silver's back.

It's not that the Lone Ranger doesn't love Silver; it's not that the
Ranger isn't Silver's friend. It's that he can switch at will from mate
to master while Silver has no choice in the matter; Silver's unacknowledged slide from pal to vehicle of transportation doesn't bother
anybody but him.

Children's serials, as you might expect, emphasize the hoped
for mutuality of the horse-rider arrangement: Silver, like Tom
Mix's Tony ("the smartest horse in the movies") and Roy Rogers'
Trigger, is a magical friend, there in time of need, always doing
his master's bidding, but disappearing like a genie back into a
bottle when more exciting business calls. In adult Westerns it is
different. The horse is not a friend won through nurture and
gentle suasion, but an occasion for proving the hero's superior
strength and cunning. Where some television shows and most B
Westerns (low-budget movies made in a few days for Saturday-
afternoon viewing) imagine a peaceable kingdom where all
beings gratefully accept their roles after a few bad characters have
been expelled, A Westerns posit a kingdom of force and conflict,
where humans and animals, men and women, bosses and under-
lings vie for dominance and define themselves by competing
with each other.

This is the world depicted in *The Big Country*, when the well-dressed, well-spoken, well-mannered Jim McKay (played by Gregory Peck) arrives at his fiancee's ranch. He lets some rowdies rough him up when he and his fiancee are driving home from the station; he refuses to fight the foreman (played by Charlton Heston) who has eyes for his girl. And when the stable hands arrange for him to ride Old Thunder, a horse obviously known for his ornery ways, he declines the gambit.

But when everyone leaves, McKay goes back to the barn and has the Mexican stableman (stereotypically plump and servile) lead Old Thunder into the corral. In the classic contest of wills between man and horse to see who will outlast the other, time after time the handsome McKay is thrown to the dust, and time after time he gets back on. Finally, he manages to hold his seat and in short order has Old Thunder behaving like a lamb. We breathe a sigh of relief.

The episode from *The Big Country* shows how men in Westerns use horses to prove their manhood—both in the sense of their superiority to other animals and in the sense of their difference from and superiority to women and lower-order males. The contest with Old Thunder dramatizes a fact already implicit in the horse-rider relation: it testifies to the man's dominion. The horse, like a colonized subject, makes a man a master. Its association with knighthood, chivalric orders, lordly privilege, and high degree reinforces the image of mastery that a man on horseback represents. That image is political through and through. In the Far West, it says, every man can be a master. Every man can dominate something, be it the landscape, other human beings, an animal, or his own body. Each time the figure of a horseman appears against the horizon, it celebrates the possibility of mastery, of self, of others, of the land, of circumstance.

Yet it isn't that simple. Though the A Western glories in the hero's power over nature and other men, it frequently does so with a kind of bitter regret, almost perversely forcing itself to count the cost of victory. Every time a horse is broken, an outlaw killed, a homestead protected, that much of the West disappears. The emotion that the taming of horses leaves behind is not so much triumph as nostalgia. Nostalgia for the Wild West, for the untamed body, for the spirit and energy conveyed by the presence of horses. In Dalton Trumbo's great screenplay for *Lonely Are the Brave,* that nostalgia becomes the Western's explicit theme.

From the very beginning, when the camera discovers the hero (Kirk Douglas) napping on the prairie with his horse, the movie equates the hero with his horse and both with everything the bureaucratic, machine-run, rule-bound modern world would deprive them of—spontaneity, beauty, freedom from rules and routines, and the right to enjoy life. Once, when he is being chased by the police, the hero has a chance to get away if he is willing to abandon his horse, Whiskey. At first, he is willing, but almost immediately changes his mind and can't go through with it, for Whiskey has been his only companion throughout his attempt to escape the vengeful representatives of a jail-like society who are pursuing him; he talks to Whiskey all the time, and as the story progresses, she grows more and more appealing. In the final scene their identification is complete. The cowboy and his horse, who have almost made it to the border despite the mechanized police effort, are hit by a truck as they cross a highway in a midnight rainstorm. As Kirk Douglas looks pathetically up into the camera, his rain-wet face like a baby's in its innocence and bewilderment, he resembles nothing so much as Whiskey—who has already been shot—beautiful, innocent, uncomprehending flesh struck down by a machine.

The physical beauty of the horse and its rider sets them apart from the other characters in the film—policemen, jail guards, sheriffs—whose uniforms reflect the regimented lives they (and the audience) lead. A beautiful palomino, sleek and plump like Kirk Douglas himself, and very frisky—Whiskey is deliberately played off against the sheriff's dog, a poor-looking mutt who pisses on the same spot at the same time every day. The human characters, of course, are played off against the hero. When the driver of the fatal truck, which was carrying toilet seats, says to a policeman on the scene, "He's not going to die, is he?" the policeman replies, "How should I know, I've got a report to write." In their comeliness and grace Kirk Douglas and Whiskey incarnate all that is desirable and precious about living things. Their appeal is to the essential blame-lessness and vulnerability of the body and to its inborn desire for pleasure and freedom.

The painfulness of watching this film brings to the surface an element of grief and suffering not at all foreign to Western film-making. The movie catches the audience in an emotional double bind, filling us with longing for a mode of life that it then declares extinct before our very eyes. It makes us love the hero and his horse and at the same time shows us that we represent the civilization that has killed them. This double bind works even more clearly in stories that dispense with the human protagonist altogether and give us only the horse to identify with.

In *The Mustangs* (1934), J. Frank Dobie tells the story of Starface, a bay stallion with a white star-shaped patch on his forehead, who regularly raided the ranches for mares to add to his band. Though he had been shot at hundreds of times, "the boldest gallant and the most magnificent thief that the Cimarron ranges had ever known," Starface had never allowed men to get close enough even to nick him with a bullet. Finally, the ranchers hire four cowboys with the best horses in the country, ordering them not to come home until they have captured the stallion or killed him. The men chase Star-face for four days until, at dawn on the fifth day, they drive him into a canyon that ends in a bluff high over the Cimarron River. Dobie writes:

> As the mustang ascended into a patch of sunshine allowed by a break in the walls on the opposite side of the canyon and they could see the sheen of light on his muscles, one of them called out, "God, look at the King of the horse world!"
>
> . . . Towering above the bench [where Starface stood] was a caprock,

without a seam or a slope in its face. . . . As the leading rider emerged
to the level, he saw Starface make his last dash.

He was headed for the open end of the bench. At the brink he gathered
his feet as if to vault the Cimarron itself, and then, without halting a
second, he sprang into space. For a flash of time, without tumbling,
he remained stretched out, terror in his streaming mane and tail, the
madness of ultimate defiance in his eyes. With him it was truly "Give
me Liberty or give me Death." (185–86)

The story makes us feel the contradiction horses in Westerns
embody by putting us in an intolerable position: up there on the
cliff with Starface, with nowhere to go but over the edge or into
the hands of the hired *mesteñeros*. We must either commit suicide
along with the horse or draw back at the last minute and by default
be associated with the men who have caused his death. In effect,
we are the monsters, the settlers, the conquerors who have tamed
and destroyed the wilderness; but we are also the horse up there on
the ledge, desperate to be free.

Lonely Are the Brave traps us in the same dilemma. Either we
take the plunge across the midnight highway, where we know
the semi is going to hit us, or we side with the men in the heli-
copters, with their two-way radios, their badges, and their forms
to fill out. By offering dead-end alternatives in both directions,
the nostalgic narrative visits on the reader/viewer the same cruelty it visits on the protagonist. Although this story longs for a
different world from the one it depicts, it doesn't offer us that
world experientially, but is complicit with the regime of pain it
criticizes by giving pain itself.

The extent to which the Western is involved with pain has not been
commented on by critics, perhaps because the critics themselves
are so habituated to this kind of pain that they just don't notice it.
But the genre is riddled with pain. *Lonely Are the Brave* puts the

audience through a psychological anguish which is the counterpart of the physical suffering the Western regularly visits on its heroes. In *One-Eyed Jacks* (1960) Marlon Brando's hand is pounded to a pulp by another man's pistol butt. In *Warlock* Richard Widmark has his hand pinned to a table by a knife which is then pulled through it. In *High Plains Drifter* Clint Eastwood is whipped to death on Main Street, in a lengthy flashback the movie cuts to several times. In *Lonely Are the Brave* Kirk Douglas is beaten up three times before he starts his desperate flight from his motorized pursuers. Gary Cooper, in *High Noon*, has to slug it out at length with a man half his age before facing Frank Miller and his gang. And so on. The physical punishment heroes take is not incidental to their role; it is constitutive of it. Prolonged and deliberate laceration of the flesh, endured without complaint, is a sine qua non of masculine achievement. It indicates the control the man can exercise over his body and his feelings. It is the human counterpart of horse breaking, only what is being broken is not the horse's will but the hero's natural emotions. The hero beats himself into submission in the same way he subdues the animal.

A movie not coincidentally entitled A *Man Called Horse* (1969) celebrates just such a triumph of the will in a way that emphasizes its most negative aspects. The hero, played by Richard Harris, a wealthy Englishman who has bought his title and is bored with life, has "come halfway round the world just to shoot another kind of bird." Captured by Sioux Indians and given to the chief's mother as a servant, he is subjected to physical abuse and social humiliation, forced to fetch wood and do other menial tasks. In protest, he announces loudly to his captors: "I AM NOT A HORSE. I AM A MAN." The Indians, naturally, call him "Horse" from then on.

The rest of the movie is about how Horse finds the meaning of life by proving his manhood to the Indians. He does this first by killing two Shoshone braves who have happened onto a berrying expedition (Horse has been set this low-level task along with the squaws), counting coup in the Indian manner by scalping them, which disgusts him but delights his captors. He has now earned the right to marry an Indian woman who has been making eyes at him, the sister of Yellow Hand (she has no name of her own). But first he must prove that he is a warrior by undergoing an ordeal. Horse declares: "I want to prove my courage. To withstand all tests of pain."

The ordeal is the climax of the movie. After standing in the blinding-hot sun all day, Horse is hung from a tent pole by the sinews of his chest, the whole tribe looking on; after enduring this silently for a long time, he is cut down and allowed to marry the girl. The point of the movie seems to be that the white man is more of a man than any of the Indians and that what makes him so is his ability to stand pain: first the pain of maltreatment and humiliation, and then the pain of the ritual ordeal. When the hero says in the beginning, "I am not a horse, I am a man," it implies that horses are fit recipients for the maltreatment he is suffering but humans are not. Yet, in order to prove that he is a man, he allows his body to be tortured, treating it as if it were a horse. The homology the film establishes— will is to body as man is to horse—is present in a less explicit form in all Western novels and films, underwriting the ethos of domination the horse-rider relationship exemplifies.

The tests of pain that heroes withstand, and the beatings and the shootings they deal out, are more or less consciously registered by the film and by the audience. But there is another level of pain recurrent in Westerns that is not consciously recognized and for that reason is even more symptomatic. I mean the pain meted out to horses. Horses are regularly whipped by stage drivers and wagoneers, forced up steep hills and down sharp ravines, driven through flooding rivers and into quagmires. They pull heavy loads in the hot sun. They are spurred and whipped by posses and escaping bandits, shot at by practically everyone—thieves, murderers, good guys, cavalry, Indians. They are frequently wounded and killed.

They are forced to jump through the plate-glass windows of banks, ridden into churches and courthouses, across wooden sidewalks, and through burning buildings. They are caught in the middle of gunfights and ridden into barren places where they must go without water or food or shelter. What horses endure in Westerns is very much like what heroes endure, except that they aren't acting voluntarily and can't defend themselves or run away.

Like the messages said to appear in television advertisements that flash before the eye so quickly you can't actually see them but absorb them without knowing it, the suffering of horses is transmitted subliminally. Animal pain, there on the screen but not consciously apprehended, imprints itself on the viewer's psychic retina in scene after scene. The effect is inchoate, a sense of something bad going on just out of range, something that shouldn't happen but that can't be attended to because other much more important events (what is happening to the hero) are occurring at the same time. The unacknowledged abuse of horses injects an element of violence into scenes where nothing else is happening, as a way of filling in the gaps between acts of violence involving humans. This persistent borderline cruelty to horses is not an epiphenomenon but is integral to the work Westerns do.

The cruelty meted out to horses is an extension of the cruelty meted out to men's bodies and emotions; the pain horses endure is an analogue of the pain the hero inflicts on himself. His impassivity, his hyperbolically reductive language ("nope," "yup"), the stillness of his body, his studied nonreaction to provocation, his poker face—these are the external signs of the ruthless suppression of feeling that marks him as "strong." The continual control he exercises over himself emotionally prepares us and him for the monumental self-discipline he will have to exert in the climactic ordeal, which will subject his body to prolonged physical suffering. The abuse of horses is part of a sadomasochistic impulse central to Westerns which aims at the successful domination of the emotions, of the fleshly mortal part of the self, and of the material world outside the body.

Frederic Remington, American, 1861–1909, "The Bronco Buster," cast
by the Roman Bronze Works, New York, New York, bronze, modelled 1909,
cast 1912, ht.: 82.6 cm. 3/4 front view.

That part of the self experienced as mortal, the body and its feelings, has already been expelled symbolically from the main action of the Western plot with the expulsion of women. In the constant spectacle of the horse's submission to human control, it continues to be manipulated, curbed, punished, and sometimes killed before our eyes.

Still from *Red River* (United Artists, 1948).
Courtesy of the Museum of Modern Art/Film Stills Archive, New York.

Cattle

5

Humane slaughter. In both the United States and Europe the desirability of stunning was recognized before the end of the 19th century. . . . Cattle may be stunned by means of a captive-bolt pistol or a pneumatic gun. Sheep and pigs may be stunned by pistol, by electric shock, or by anesthetizing in a carbon dioxide chamber. After World War II, compressed-air stunners were commonly used for cattle and gas chambers for smaller animals.

Cattle slaughter. After stunning, the carcass is vertically suspended by one or both hindlegs, and the carotid arteries and jugular veins are severed. The carcass is then skinned with an air-operated or electrically operated skinning knife. In old or small operations this is accomplished with the aid of a "stationary bed" on which a pointed stick helps hold the carcass on its back on the floor. Large modern plants use "rail dressing," employing platforms and hide-pullers.

Evisceration and splitting are similar to methods used in hog slaughter. Shrouding, performed on many beef carcasses, involves soaking a muslin cloth in warm water and stretching it tightly over the outside surface, securing it with metal pins. The carcasses are then placed in the cooler; and, after 24 hours, the shrouds are removed, and the carcass fat remains smooth and trim.

"Food Processing," *The New Encyclopaedia Britannica,*
vol. 19, pp. 356–57.

In *High Plains Drifter* one of the villains, who've just been let out of jail, says to the others in a moment of vicious hilarity, "When we get to Lago, I'll have the mayor's horse, fried and barbecued." We know this is a joke and suitable for a villain because in our society it's all right to eat cattle but not all right to eat horses, at least not under most circumstances. Such a distinction, when you give it a little thought (which Westerns do not), loses its self-evident quality. Why is it OK to eat cattle and not horses? Why do we keep cats and dogs as pets but behave differently toward, say, raccoons, using their pelts for fur coats, while treating rabbits both as pets *and* as food and clothing? Why isn't it all right to barbecue the mayor's horse? Why doesn't Roy Rogers eat Trigger?

Once you start thinking about horses in Westerns, sooner or later you end up thinking about animals in general, especially cattle, a subject that leads to considerations most people would rather avoid. The way we behave toward animals stems partly from the fact that they occupy mutually exclusive categories in our thinking: person and thing, organism and machine, companion and slave, friend and food. Animals are both like us (person, organism, companion, friend) and not like us, treated as if they were objects (steaks, vehicles, lab specimens). That's why it's hard to read descriptions like the ones printed above of the process of slaughtering cattle.

There is no sense to be made of the contrary labels—and functions—we assign to animals without getting entangled in debates about the propriety of people's ingrained tastes and habits (e.g., eating meat, wearing leather, using products tested on animals), or becoming embroiled in arguments that threaten to upset most people's unquestioned beliefs about the uniqueness of being human (e.g., having language, being self-conscious, making moral choices). For the difficulty of thinking about animals has to do primarily with the slipperiness of who "we" are, as opposed to who we are not (e.g., two-legged vs. four-legged, rational vs. instinctual).

Or, to put it in a slightly different way, the problem stems from our difficulty in deciding how far and in what directions we are willing to extend a sense of identification, a difficulty in deciding where "we" begin and end. The gray area begins inside the body and extends outward from there. Do we identify ourselves with our minds or with our bodies? With certain thoughts (or feelings) rather than with others? With an eternal soul? Do we identify ourselves with our possessions (a car, a pet, a wedding ring, a book we've written), with our friends, members of our own family, people who belong to the same region, class, profession, nationality, gender, ethnic group, race? Do we identify ourselves with other species and, if so, which ones—the "higher" mammals, dolphin but not tuna? With other life forms? The universe? Where do we draw the line between self and not-self? And do we draw it in different places at different times?

It's not my intention to go deeply here into the highly charged issues these questions raise, but rather to point out how the assumptions that underlie our behavior with respect to animals are fundamental to the Western and crucially shape its vision of the heroic life.

I suggested earlier that the body of the hero is the analogue of the horse he rides. What happens to the horse happens to the rider, and vice versa. The politics of the horse-rider relationship, in which the horse is subordinate to the rider, is reflected in the intrapsychic politics the Western sets up between the body and the will. The body is an instrument, designed to do the will of its master, schooled to obey commands without demur, no matter how painful or violative of its natural function they may be. This model is reproduced in even starker form in men's behavior toward cattle in Western movies. For cattle in Westerns are not broken and ridden, they are raised exclusively to be killed for food that humans eat.

Economically cattle are the basis of the way of life that Westerns represent, but if anything they are even more invisible than horses are, in the sense of not being seen for themselves, or as they would see themselves. With few exceptions (usually scenes of the branding or rescuing of calves), they are seen only from the viewpoint of their utility for humans: as factors in an economic scheme, as physical obstacles to be contended with in a heroic undertaking, or as the contested prize in an economic struggle. Although cattle are everywhere in Westerns, in the sense that their existence supports the livelihood the characters depend on, they are basically ignored. The reason for this is the same as the reason why it's hard to find out where stockyards are located in the United States or to find accounts of what happens to cattle between the time they are raised and the time their flesh appears in the supermarket. Cattle exist, from a human point of view, in order to die and become meat, and it's hard for people to look at that fact very closely.

Nevertheless it is a fact that has a profound influence on the way people live. The way people treat the world around them—animals, the land, other human beings—reveals something about themselves. This is an underlying theme in one of the greatest of Western movies, Howard Hawkes's classic *Red River*. The movie begins when Thomas Dunson, played by John Wayne, breaks away from the wagon train he has been traveling with and sets out with his friend, an older man named Nadine Groot (played by Walter Brennan), to look for land south of the Red River. He bids good-bye to his sweetheart, Fen, who begs to go with him, turns a deaf ear to the pleas of his companions, and heads resolutely south. Dunson's ruthless abandonment of people who both need and love him, here at the beginning, sets the pattern for his entrepreneurial ventures from this point on. He and Groot are attacked by Indians, one of whom Dunson stabs to death in the waters of the Red River. The next day, he and Groot find a young boy who is the sole survivor of an Indian attack that has wiped out the wagon train they deserted (good-bye fiancee and friends). Dunson knocks the boy down to teach him a lesson about not trusting strangers, but privately admits to Groot, "He'll do." (This testing inflicts a miniature version of heroic suffering; the boy who can take punches is good material.)

He becomes, in effect, Dunson's adoptive son. The boy, whose name is Matthew Garth, has a cow with him which they'll need to start a herd. This cow, the source of all Dunson's wealth, is virtually ignored.

When Dunson arrives at the spot where he's decided to put his ranch, he kills one of the outriders of the Mexican don who owns the territory and lays claim to it for himself. He boasts that in a few years the whole range will be covered with cattle—his. Fourteen years pass, and Dunson's prediction materializes. Much is made of how hard he's worked for this. The range is covered with cattle, but there's no way to sell them; the markets are too far away, and the ranchers are going broke. So Dunson decides to do the impossible: drive his cattle a thousand miles to the nearest rail head, something no one has ever done before. He takes not only his own cattle but those of the other ranchers in his district, whom he more or less bullies into the deal, promising them ten dollars a head if he makes it.

Dunson sets out on the drive with Matt as second in command (he's now a handsome young Civil War veteran, played by Montgomery Clift). Nadine Groot drives the chuck wagon. Hawkes films the drive in an epic manner, emphasizing the historic nature of the enterprise, the danger, the uncertainty, the raw energy of the cowboy recruits, the huge, lumbering mass of animals, the dust, dirt, commotion, sweat, and grueling physical hardship of the journey. They are beset by difficulties: rain and cold, short rations and long hours. There is a stampede in which a man is killed and cattle and food are lost. The men grow mutinous. Dunson kills a man who draws on him. The men grumble even more. Dunson's response is to drive them harder. The food is terrible; there's no coffee. They work into the dark and get up before daybreak. Hard as he drives the men, Dunson drives himself even harder. For several nights running, Dunson gets no sleep at all. He's wounded in a fight and drinks to kill the pain. Matt pleads with him to let up on himself and the men. Dunson refuses.

Meanwhile, the cattle are always present, being driven through all kinds of weather, over the rolling plains, across rivers, on and on. They are photographed so that we almost never see their faces; as the camera shows them to us, they are a living stream, slow, cumbersome, potentially dangerous but ultimately docile, lowing their protests ineffectually against the journey, stumbling along.

When Dunson threatens to hang two men who have tried to get away, the hands finally rebel and Matt takes over. He gives Dunson a grub stake and leaves him behind to fend for himself. The ordeal continues. When a scout brings news of a wagon train ahead where there are "women and coffee," Matt allows everyone to stop a while but not for long. Not even the charms of the beautiful Tess Millay (played by Joanne Dru) are enough to keep Matt there. He has too much of the old man in him.

When they get to Abilene there is general rejoicing. The townspeople have been longing for the arrival of a herd like this; the cattle flood the streets. Dunson arrives on the scene. There are some tense moments when it looks like Matt and Dunson might kill each other, but after a brief fistfight, they become friends again. Dunson advises Matt to marry Tess, gives him a half interest in the ranch, and promises to change the brand, which had a D for Dunson and two lines for the Red River, to D, two lines, and an M. The music swells, marking the happy conclusion.

The movie is rich in symbols that radiate in many directions, but the central point is simple. Nothing gets in Dunson's way. Not his friends, not his sweetheart, not the Indians, not the Mexicans, not the rebellious hands, not his old pal Groot who scolds him repeatedly, not the rivers, not the land, not the thousands of cattle, not even his own body. They are all a means to an end, the realization of his purpose. The movie criticizes his persistence but ultimately sees it as heroic. Everyone benefits from it in the end. The ranchers make a profit, the hands get paid, the town of Abilene and the railroad are in business, Matt inherits half the ranch, Tess gets Matt, and Dunson gets to be a hero. Everyone is better off than they were before—everyone, that is, but the cattle. They get to be herded onto boxcars and taken to the slaughterhouse in Chicago. "Good beef for hungry people," as Dunson puts it. The film takes account of the hero's excess in driving relentlessly toward his goal but never makes the connection between that drive and the driving of cattle.

The cattle are the film's unconscious. They surround the characters, often dominate the screen, pervade the atmosphere with the quiet, massive strength of their bodies, the slow, throbbing presence of their lives. Yet in some profound way they are totally unnoticed, even though they are a continual focus of energy and attention throughout the movie. The film's title, *Red River*, repeats the name of the river the characters must cross to get the cattle to market. And the name of the river refers, presumably, to its color. But besides the river and its color, the title of the film evokes the land's fertility, the blood of the Indians who gave up the land, the blood of the Mexicans from whom it was also taken, the blood of all the others who died to make Dunson's victory possible (the hands, his former companions on the wagon train, his sweetheart), but most of all—and inevitably, though it is never thought of in this way—it stands for the cattle. A river of living beings whose death is the uncounted cost of success. They constitute the story's economic base, they are its *raison d'être*, and they provide it, at twenty-one dollars a head, with a triumphant resolution. The sacrifice of their lives underwrites everything. *Red River* ends with the prospect of a gigantic river of blood, but that river is kept off-screen because it has no place in the consciousness of filmmakers or of the society they cater to.

That the film is rarely seen this way, and the history of the West seldom written from this point of view, is evidence of our cultural blind spot when it comes to animals. The extermination of the Indians has finally been faced by American historians, and the rise of ecological consciousness has made us aware of the near-extinction of the buffalo and the plundering of the land. But cattle cannot be seen or thought about in these ways yet because their invisibility is necessary if our society is to carry on some of its taken-for-granted activities: eating beef, wearing leather, using animal products, and continuing to support the huge and lucrative cattle industry—blood for money. In the case of *Red River*, our blindness to the cattle makes possible a feeling of accomplishment at the end of the movie, of joy and relief when the men finally make it to Abilene. The sense of satisfaction in work accomplished, the financial reward, the founding of a dynasty, the fulfillment of a dream, the symbolic settling of a region, the opening of a vast new market—these triumphs all ride, so to speak, on the backs of the herd. In order for the story to work, we must believe at some level, in no matter how dim or incompletely imagined a way, that it is all right to make cattle walk a thousand miles to be herded onto boxcars, transported to stockyards, slaughtered, made into meat for human consumption and into dollars for people in the cattle business. On our acceptance of this process the entire story depends.

While *Red River* openly celebrates human courage and endurance, and is a haunting, powerful rendition of some of the great themes of Western novels and films, it also tacitly endorses practices of enslavement and massacre that neither the film nor its audience takes cognizance of. We do not recognize these practices as such because our culture has trained us not to. Habitually and self-protectively we turn away from what we cannot bear to see. Meanwhile, for the animals, as Isaac Bashevis Singer has said, every day is Treblinka. Lending their energy and life to the moving picture, epitomizing its goal, yet hardly ever recognized for what they are— sentient beings like ourselves, capable of pleasure and pain—cattle are an enabling condition of Western narratives. They *cannot* be seen for themselves. To do so would make the Western impossible.

To see animals as they see themselves would make the Western impossible not only because cattle and horses are economically essential to the society the Western depicts but because the relation humans have to them is the same one they have to their own bodies and emotions. To see animals differently would require human beings to see themselves differently also. Thomas Dunson drives his body the same way he drives his cattle. These are the terms on which he achieves success. Like the hero of *A Man Called Horse*, Dunson treats himself like a brute and in so doing is understood to be showing extraordinary willpower and determination. There is no sense that such treatment is degrading or injurious, that it might stem from insensitivity or lack of compassion. Thus, in a strange way, to recognize the suffering of animals would be to undermine the terms in which heroism is conceived. For if deliberately inflicting pain on sentient beings reflects a callous, unmerciful approach to life, then perhaps the hero's mortification of himself is not so admirable as we've been encouraged to believe.

The invisibility of cattle in Westerns—the invisibility, that is, of their terrible suffering at human hands—and the celebration of the hero's pain are intricately linked. Both depend on an instrumentalization of the body, turning living flesh into pieces of meat. The hero, who must take pain silently, learns to deaden his natural reactions to pain in order to survive his ordeal. And the habitual numbing of himself makes it easier for him to inflict pain on others, as Dunson does, and even to kill them when necessary. When Nadine Groot chides his boss repeatedly with the words "You wuz wrong, Mister Dunson," he is criticizing Dunson's insentience in pushing his men beyond their endurance, a form of stupidity, ultimately, which leads to Dunson's temporary downfall.

In *Red River* society is rescued from the tyrant's unbearably heavy hand by his adoptive son, who represents a gentler dispensation. But when Matthew Garth takes over it is a change only of degree, not of kind. The disciplinary order Dunson stands for is in full sway at the end of the film: Matthew has reenacted his earlier rebellion against the old king in his concluding fistfight with Dunson, which ends in an embrace, and authority is duly passed down from father to son. They are now co-owners of the ranch; together they will make the decisions, hire the hands, give the orders, drive the cattle, sell them to the dealers, and see that they produce a profit. The numbed awareness is still in effect, though it is no longer perceived by the audience, who acquiesce in this new version of the old regime. The numbness is most in evidence where it is least able to be apprehended—in the treatment of the cattle. At the end of the movie the cattle are waiting in the holding pens where the sun beats down and the manure piles up. Our acceptance, in the softer figure of Matt, of the regime Thomas Dunson embodies signals our acceptance of the attitudes that rule the world Westerns represent. A world that rewards striving to get ahead at other people's expense, single-minded pursuit of material goals, strategic or rote mortification of the flesh, unvoiced suffering. And it includes the daily slaughter of millions of animals and a smell that rises from the stockyards and the slaughterhouses, a smell that does not make it onto celluloid or into print, and seldom reaches the nostrils of anyone outside the environs of the principal livestock markets: Chicago, established 1865; Kansas City, 1871; St. Louis, 1872; Omaha, 1884; Denver, 1886; Sioux City, 1887; St. Joseph, 1893; Wichita, 1893; Fort Worth, 1902.

We are ignorant of stockyards and do not think about what goes on inside slaughterhouses because to do so would involve us in contradictions we cannot emotionally sustain. But to the extent that some awareness of animal suffering is unavoidable, we have been schooled to regard the expression of sympathy or pity as sentimental. (The standard definition of sentimental is, "indulging in excessive or unnecessary feeling in response to a negligible stimulus.") This view of sentimentality does not exist independently of the Western; it's an attitude the Western (though not, of course, the Western alone) educates us to. In the course of providing a set of master images that tell men how to behave in society, Westerns teach men that they must take pain and give it, without flinching. The education of the hero and of the hero's audience moves in the direction of induration, hardening. We are taught not to cry out or show that we care. For to show that your heart is not hard, to cry when you feel pain, your own or someone else's, is sentimental—indulging in excessive or unnecessary feeling in response to a negligible stimulus—in other words, soft, womanish, emotional, the very qualities the Western hero must get rid of to be a man.

The Western schools people to scorn the expression of sympathy for pain because it needs an interdiction against such expressions to keep itself in business. You can't have people worrying about what branding feels like in stories where ranching is the main livelihood. But the interdiction against sentimentality does not apply to the suffering of animals alone; it's needed to support the image of manhood the genre underwrites.

The ability to give pain and take it stoically is built into the disciplinary model of child rearing that Alice Miller outlines in her study of the roots of violence in Western culture, *For Your Own Good: Hidden Cruelty in Child-Rearing and the Roots of Violence.* Her analysis of why parents treat children as they do highlights the self-perpetuating, involuntary cycle of cruelty in human relations which the Western aids and abets. In discussing the reason why parents punish children for actions that are natural and innocent, Miller writes:

> A person [who] becomes a father . . . will be confronted with a situation that threatens the whole structure he has taken such pains to erect: he sees before him a child full of life, sees how a human being is meant to be, how *he* could have been if obstacles hadn't been placed in his way. But his fears are soon activated: this cannot be allowed to happen. If the child were allowed to stay as he is, wouldn't that mean that the

father's sacrifices and self-denial weren't really necessary? . . . Without meaning to and without realizing it, the father treat[s] his child just as cruelly as he treat[s] the child within himself. (94–95)

"The child within himself" is the key here. Miller is saying that people (in this case, a father) treat others the way they treat themselves, and that they treat themselves the way they have been treated. The father who punishes the child for spontaneity is repeating what was once done to him and what he has long since learned to do to himself (the child within). It's easy to see, then, how the question of punishment central to the parent-child relation is also central to the Western. The hero's demonstration of mastery over himself is proof that he has successfully internalized the dictates of parental control. He has successfully subdued the child. And his mastery of himself makes him want to master others as he has been mastered. In this respect, and despite its reputation as an escapist, adolescent genre, the Western can be seen as a powerful reinforcer of socialization, in that it keeps in place structures of domination and control, of others and of the self. The hero suffers, makes himself suffer, causes suffering in others because this is what he has been trained to do.

Red River provides an excellent mini-case in point. Thomas Dunson punches the boy, Matthew Garth, the first time he meets him, to teach him a lesson (never trust a stranger) "for his own good." This blow might stand, metaphorically, for the passing on of pain from generation to generation that Miller's study describes. The rest of the film shows Dunson inflicting constant pain on himself and others, in response, presumably, to the blows that knocked him down when he was growing up.

In the process by which people learn to give and receive blows in Westerns, animals play a central though unobserved part. The horses and cattle that men variously drive, command, subdue, and often kill—though they sometimes rescue and love them as well—are an analogue to the child within. With their physicality, their innocence, their helplessness to defend themselves, their spontaneity and wordlessness, horses and cattle are the exterior representatives of the old longings, needs, and urges of the physical and emotional body that still exist inside the hero. Given the code of behavior he must live up to, though, these impulses don't stand a chance. The slaughter of ten thousand cattle that awaits at the conclusion of *Red River* fulfills what the heroism of the drive has already begun.

Still from *True Grit*, starring John Wayne (Paramount Pictures, 1969).
Courtesy of the Museum of Modern Art/Film Stills Archive, New York.

Dry-Gulched ☆
A Reckoning

6

When we stand back and look at the picture I have been drawing, what becomes obvious is that the Western, a genre that in many ways exists in order to fill its audience's need to be reunited with nature, is also engaged in suppressing and curtailing and in some cases extinguishing the very life source it so eagerly seeks to repossess. Through the cruel treatment of the hero and of animals, through the "drive," the spontaneous, exuberant, fleshly, and passionate part of human beings is a continual object of punishment, manipulation, and control. This tendency becomes all the more striking and re-markable when we consider a strange intersection or overlap that occurs, in this connection, between Westerns and the sentimental novels they arose in order to refute.

In the intrapsychic politics the Western sets up, the body and the emotions have no "rights," as it were, no voice; like the animals, they do not speak. The same is true in a certain respect of the sentimental novel. Though the protagonist was allowed the outlet of tears, her heroism lay in her capacity for selfless renunciation of her desires. She had to relinquish her aspirations for social position, for wealth, for luxury and comfort, for congenial occupations, for family, friends, companions, for dignity and respect, indeed, for mortal succor of any kind. Beyond this, she had to renounce some of her deepest feelings, particularly the outrage that welled up in her spontaneously when the world hit her after she was down. The heroine's claim on our admiration, therefore, lay primarily in her ability to withstand a tremendous amount of psychological suffering. Her message to us, as Martha Vicinus succinctly put it, was "suffer and be still." That, oddly enough, is the same thing Westerns are saying to their male audiences.

The sentimental heroine, always unjustly treated, was forbidden to show her anger; the Western hero, always subjected to duress, is forbidden to register his pain. Both genres replicate the conditions Miller specifies in her analysis of childhood trauma as leading to "pathological development," where she repeatedly stresses that

> it is not the trauma itself that is the source of illness but the unconscious, repressed hopeless despair over not being allowed to give expression to what one has suffered and the fact that one is not allowed to show and is unable to experience feelings of rage, anger, humiliation, despair, helplessness, and sadness. . . . Pain over the frustration one has suffered is nothing to be ashamed of, nor is it harmful. It is a natural, human reaction. However, if it is verbally or nonverbally forbidden or even stamped out by force . . . then natural development is impeded and the conditions for pathological development are created. (259)

The revolution brought about by the substitution of the Western for the sentimental novel effects a change of gender and of costume, of narrative style, characters, and mise-en-scène; it replaces one set of ultimate beliefs with another, gets rid of organized religion, class distinctions, and the more obvious artifacts of high culture; but something that may turn out to be more crucial than any of these remains the same: the disciplinary model of heroism held up to the reading audience for emulation. The painful experience the protagonist undergoes in both cases, the pattern of self-renunciation each is required to live out, the regimen of silence imposed where expression is most needed, and the equation of this repression with the highest integrity and authenticity—this recipe for heroic selfhood remains unchanged from the nineteenth to the twentieth century.

One has to ask why. What social need is there so deep, so pervasive, and so hidden that it insists on this continuity of character in narrative traditions so totally opposed to each other in all obvious ways? The question reverberates in so many quarters that a single answer is impossible. But here is an observation. For both male and female heroes, gender patrols the borders of expression, keeping men and women from protesting their lot by threatening them with the label of deviance. Women cannot express their rage because to do so marks them as unfeminine. Men cannot register their pain because to do so marks them as unmanly. The gender system works to enforce codes of behavior that are, in their different ways, excruciating. No police force in the world could exact a stricter obedience to these codes than sentimental heroines and Western heroes learn to impose on themselves. The most effective motivator of human action is not force or money or even power; it is what other people will think.

With an irony so deep it evokes pity, the Western struggles and strains to cast out everything feminine, but in doing so only embeds itself more firmly in the gender system. In the effort to free itself from the suffocating restrictions of Victorian social mores—temperance, sexual repression, elaborate dress codes, Anglophile gentility, evangelical piety, and the worship of domesticity and highbrow culture for their own sakes—the Western paints itself into another kind of corner. Striving to be the opposite of women, the male heroes restrict themselves to a pitiably narrow range of activities. They can't read or dance or look at pictures. They can't play. They can't rest. They can't look at the flowers. They can't cook or sew or keep house, or carry on a conversation of more than a couple of sentences. They can't not know something, or ask someone else the way. They can't daydream or fantasize or play the fool. They can't make mistakes.

When Joey calls out at the end of *Shane*, and the call echoes, "Come back, Shane!" we want Shane to come back just as much as he does. But suppose Shane *had* come back and had gotten

Marian Starrett away from Joe, Sr. What would it have been like to live with him? Shane was a man of few words, mysterious, catlike, sexually appealing, with something a little deadly in the background. The example isn't easy because Alan Ladd was so attractive in the role, but give it a moment's speculation. What would it be like to spend long days with this edgy, introverted person, with hair-trigger reflexes and an undigestible past? How much did Shane like living with himself?

The gender system catches Western heroes in a trap. The free, wild prairie promises liberation from stuffy interiors and bad family scenarios, but the type of heroism it seems to legitimize doesn't produce a very viable person, a person who enjoys living with himself and other people. Silence, the will to dominate, and unacknowledged suffering aren't a good recipe for happiness or companionability. The model of heroism Westerns provide may help men to make a killing in the stock market, but it doesn't provide much assistance when they go home for dinner at night.

Case Studies

II

Portrait of Owen Wister, c. 1898.
Courtesy of the Historical Society of Pennsylvania, Society Portrait Collection.

The Virginian ☆
Wister's Mother

7

Now what should authority do upon these free plains, this wilderness of
do-as-you-please, where mere breathing the air was like inebriation?
  Owen Wister, *Lin McLean*

Near the end of Owen Wister's *Virginian* (1902), the hero shoots
and kills an outlaw named Trampas in a main street duel that became the typical climax of Western movies for the next seventy-five
years. Just before the shoot-out something happens that is equally
central to the Western's subsequent popularity. The hero's
sweetheart, Molly, declares that she won't marry him if he risks
his life against Trampas, but he does it anyway, and she takes him
back.

 The structure of the incident—in which a man defies a woman's
wishes by fighting with another man, and wins, without alienating
her—is central to the Western genre as a whole. But the meaning
of the scene and the reason for its prevalence in Westerns was never
clear to me until I became acquainted with the life of Owen Wister.
It was Wister's relation to his mother that provided the clue. Not
only *The Virginian* but crucial aspects of the Western as a whole
made a new kind of sense when considered in light of the hero's
relation to maternal authority.

Historically, I've argued, the Western is a reaction against a female-dominated tradition of popular culture; it buries its origins by excluding everything domestic from its worldview. This phenomenon has a psychological parallel. The form heroism takes in the Western can best be understood by seeing it as a reaction to something else: the hero's invisible past, the time in his life when he was an infant in his mother's arms. Why does the climactic scene in Westerns so often occur in opposition to a woman's will? To answer that question it is useful to know something of the life of Sarah Butler Wister, whose son gave the genre its classic form. She was a woman who, according to Wister's biographer, Darwin Payne, was worthy of a book herself.

Sarah Butler Wister was the daughter of Fanny Kemble, the famous British actress who married a Philadelphian, Pierce Butler, with whom she did not get along. Butler came from a family of former slaveholders and owned some large plantations in South Carolina and Georgia, whose management fell to him in time. He played the flute, had a taste for fine wines, and conducted numerous affairs with women while he was married. His wife—an international celebrity, intellectual, and moralist, a person of extremely strong character and decided views—had already established a prominent social position through her brilliant acting career. Revolted by her husband's womanizing and even more by the treatment of the slaves on his Carolina and Georgia plantations (which she described in *Journal of a Residence on a Georgian Plantation in 1838–1839*), she eventually refused to live with him and spent a good part of her time traveling. She took the children along.

Her eldest daughter, Sarah, Owen's mother, was a highly intelligent, gifted, and beautiful girl who tended to side with her mother in the battles that raged between her parents. Her own marriage seems not to have been much happier than theirs. After marrying

Portrait of Sarah Butler Wister, c. 1907.
Courtesy of the Historical Society of Pennsylvania, Society Portrait Collection.

a Philadelphia physician named Owen Jones Wister, she wrote anonymously on cultural affairs for the *Atlantic Monthly,* the *North American Review*, and other periodicals. During her early married life, she was a good friend of Henry James. Very active socially, she traveled, entertained, and kept up with her set, which was the American aristocracy of the day.

In middle age, Sarah Butler Wister was subject to depression. Darwin Payne sums up her problem succinctly:

> Sarah Wister suffered from a strong intellect with no place to put it. Her husband, a physician, was too practical for her. She disdained him for his practicality. She was flighty, nervous, and interested in poetry and music rather than daily realities. She sprang from a troubled marriage herself and a mother who was not a strong nurturing type. She was a most intriguing character, worthy herself of a book. (Payne, personal correspondence)

Described by Henry James as "a beautiful woman with fierce energy in a slender frame," Sarah Wister directed her resources of intellect and intensity on her son, Owen, recording meticulously her attempts to guide his growth in a journal she kept entitled "The Early Years of a Child of Promise." Like other people who set extremely high standards for themselves, Sarah Wister was very demanding of Owen. In Payne's words, "she criticized virtually everything he did."

It is this aspect of Sarah Wister—her critical voice—that made her such a powerful influence on her son. (After the publication of *The Virginian*, she wrote him a long letter consisting of detailed criticisms of the novel.) She is installed in his mind forever as sitting judge, internal censor, arbiter of all things visible and invisible. Whether he went with or against them, her tastes and opinions affected his; her aristocratic personality and manners would blend with his, especially in later life.

Meanwhile, his mother's unused energy and thwarted talents took their toll on everyone around her. Her behavior toward servants and people she hired to work for her was at times imperious and demanding. During a visit to Paris, prescribed for her nerves, she announced calmly to Owen that henceforth her life would consist of nothing but odds and ends. Owen was so devastated by these and other pronouncements that he wrote to his father: "it will be a relief to herself, & ought to be to all who love her, when Death closes her story" (Payne, 59).

Sarah's deep psychological distress was too much for Owen; he throws the blame for her suffering on his father, but he must have felt implicated in it himself—as cause, scapegoat, or possible future legatee—or he would not have come so close to saying he wished she were dead. A statement later in the letter reveals how trying Owen's relationship to both his parents was. He says that since neither his father nor his mother is likely to derive much pleasure from life henceforth, "I will try to remember that it must come out of mine, & shape my ways accordingly" (Payne, 59). The pressure Wister felt from his parents to make their pleasure come out of his life shaped his life conclusively. Wister struggled to remain connected to his parents and to be an independent person at the same time. His desire to please them was a crucial determinant of his marriage and career. So much so that in his choice of vocation he tried to give up his own will entirely.

When he wrote that letter home from Paris, Sarah was there for her nerves, but Owen had come to study music. At Harvard he'd taken composition and counterpoint, and his work had already been praised by American musicians; it was time to study abroad. But his father, who was extremely unhappy at this prospect, had demanded that Wister get a second opinion of his musical talents from Franz Liszt, a friend of the family. It was a test.

Wister went to see Liszt, played for him, and Liszt endorsed his musical aspirations, writing to Fanny Kemble that Wister had "*un talent prononcé.*" Marmontel, the French composer with whom Wister had been studying in Paris, seconded this, saying he had done "original work." So Wister wrote to his father in the strongest terms reaffirming his decision to make music his profession. In reply, his father refused to pay for any lessons after the following spring and went about obtaining a position for his son with a financial firm in Boston.

What Wister did next affected him, I believe, for the rest of his life. He decided to return to the United States and go into business. When his father relented a few months later and said he was willing to support a musical career, Wister not only did not change his mind, he wrote back, "I have not only merely accepted what you wish, but *I wish it myself. . .*" (Payne, 58). In a moment of deep self-betrayal, Wister turns his back on his talents, his achievements, his dreams, his desires, and does what his father wishes. More than that, he tries to become his father: "I have not only merely accepted what you wish, but *I wish it myself.*" He returns to Boston and becomes a clerk for the firm of Lee and Higginson.

Not surprisingly, this arrangement didn't last. While going to his dull job in Boston, Wister began work on a novel called "A Wise Man's Son," about a young man born to be an artist whose father forced him into business. At the same time, his health started to break down. He began to have recurrent attacks of Bell's palsy, a nerve disease in which part of the face becomes paralyzed. And when William Dean Howells, to whom Wister sent the novel asking for an opinion, told him never to show the novel to a publisher because it contained "hard swearing, hard drinking, and too much knowledge of good and evil," Wister's health collapsed.

Crushed by two father figures, his own father and Howells, Wister now proceeded to consult a third, the novelist-physician S. Weir Mitchell. This man, Sarah Butler's longtime and devoted admirer, who had sent her to Paris for her nerves, advised Wister to go west for his. For a while, the prescription worked. At the VR Ranch on Deer Creek in central Wyoming, Wister slept outdoors in a tent, bathed in the icy creek every morning, spent hours in the saddle, hunted, fished, and worked in the roundup, helping to brand calves, castrate bulls, and deliver foals. Inside three weeks he was fully recovered. He stayed all summer.

For Wister the West was the site of physical well-being and emotional rebirth, a place where it was possible to heal old wounds, forget old wrongs, recover strength, and start again. Better yet, it was a place where one could swear and drink and know good and evil, free from the sharp surveillance of one's elders, a place where those who had remained boys for reasons beyond their control could become men. Above all, it was a place for self-transformation, for a second chance.

Wister's letters back home emphasized how much his mother would have hated the West, especially the necessity of associating at close quarters with all kinds of people. For him, he said, the West was "like Genesis." It was the place where a new breed of men was coming into being, where tradition meant nothing and the weak were being winnowed out by the processes of evolution. Wister's references to birth and strength and his insistence that the West was the opposite of everything his mother stood for tell the story plainly: the West was Wister's birthplace as an independent being. In place of the rebellion against his parents Wister never acted out, there was Wyoming.

Wister created himself and his vocation out of the experiences he had on his trips West. Though he had to leave Wyoming in order to enroll in Harvard Law School in the fall (that was the plan he worked out when it was clear his job with Lee and Higginson was going nowhere), he still returned to the West repeatedly in the summers and began to write, first short stories and essays, published singly, and then collected, and finally the novel that made him famous, *The Virginian*.

But becoming an author did not provide Wister with a happy ending to his own story. His life remained complicated and contradictory, shadowed by a sense of unacted desires. This sense of unlived possibilities was recognized and articulated by Wister himself at just about the time he first went to Wyoming. On a scrap of paper entitled "Confession" he wrote:

> Were I surer of my powers,—or rather were my powers surer—I think I should not now be in America, but wandering with musicians and other disreputable people—having kicked over all traces. [But] a fortunate grain of common sense self knowledge . . . says "You're too nearly like other people to do more than appreciate & sympathize with revolution"—thus I remain conventional & am saved from fiasco. (Payne, 78)

Whether Wister was in fact saved from fiasco is a question. After his marriage to Mary Channing Wister, a second cousin on his father's side, known as Molly, and after the astoundingly successful publication of *The Virginian*, the problems that had sent him west in the first place resurfaced. For Wister, according to Malcolm Bell, Jr., "the first decade of the new century was marked by illness at home and by frequent periods of illness, depression, recovery, or rest away from Molly and their children" (471). One Wister scholar, Colin Keeney, has concluded from an extensive study of Wister's unedited journals that Wister may have been an alcoholic. At any rate, according to Bell, Wister "was unable to be husband, father, or author with any persistence." The love of a woman and the acceptance of domesticity did not work out as anticipated. And the reasons are apparent in *The Virginian*. Semiconsciously, in the novel, Wister tells a double story, the surface one of glamour and success and an understory of unhappiness hidden deep within.

The Virginian is incredibly romantic on the surface. It has the qualities of a dream come true, which was what the West had been for Wister, at least for a while. The Virginian initiates the narrator of the story (an Eastern tenderfoot much like the young Wister) into Western ways, plays a series of practical jokes on various people, outwits a bunch of rebellious cowboys he's in charge of, successfully woos and wins the heroine, kills the villain, and catches and hangs some rustlers—one of whom is his best friend, Steve.

Despite the dark tinge of this last incident, the novel's tone is lighthearted and entertaining. The Virginian and his pals are like grown-up versions of Tom Sawyer and Huck Finn: they've kicked over the traces, lit out for the territory where there's no one to watch over them, and are having the time of their lives. The romance and idealization of this story, concentrated in the hero and heroine, are what we see first and what we tend to remember in the end, despite everything.

"The fringed leathern chaparreros, the cartridge belt, the flannel shirt, the knotted scarf at the neck, these things . . . worn by this man now standing by her door, . . . seemed to radiate romance" (82). Under that delicious drawl—he says "hawss" and "laig" and "seh"—beneath the gentle manner and southern courtesy ("I'd like for yu' to go ridin' mighty well") runs a lava flow of sex. "In his eye, in his face, in his step, in the whole man, there dominated a something potent to be felt" (17): the Virginian is the sexiest thing on two legs. Tender on the outside and fierce underneath, infinitely patient and gentle toward the good people and ruthless toward the bad, the hero is irresistible.

His sweetheart, Molly, is just like him but in reverse. All sprightly wit on the outside, and inside vulnerability itself. When she rescues the Virginian after he's been wounded by Indians, he says to her, "You have got to be the man through all this mess." Molly is a man and a woman rolled into one, and therefore perfect. Soft *and* spunky. Her first two names—Molly Stark—mean softness and strength.

Beneath their cowboy and schoolmarm costumes the Virginian and Molly are recognizable types who perfectly enact the most conventional social expectations: he rough-hewn but courteous, she well educated but spunky, they articulate the desires of our hearts. And the setting of the West, the world of crystal light the moment after creation, allows them to seem possible. Their story, the story of heterosexual paradise in which ideal man and ideal woman meet and fall in love and mate, and in which he goes on to be rich and successful and she has lots of kids, is the one Wister wants to believe in. The reality is another matter.

Getting to that reality is a matter of peeling away layers: first the fiction of the hero's happy relation to women, then the notion of his natural ascendancy in the social order, and finally the idea that, having succeeded as a hero, he must be happy with himself.

The signs that *The Virginian* is not the idyll it pretends to be are all over, once you start looking for them. But the first strong signal that something is wrong comes in an early chapter about a hen named Em'ly who goes crazy. The chapter seems to have nothing to do with anything—to be just a little *jeu d'esprit*, put in for amusement's sake. What it has to do with, in fact, are Wister's feelings toward the female sex. Given the evidence of this bizarre episode, these feelings are so hostile and twisted that they cannot be expressed in any but an oblique and displaced form, perhaps because Wister was never able to express them directly in his own life—or even acknowledge their existence.

The relevant biographical context for the anecdote lies in the fact that Wister's wife, Molly, referred to by a friend as a "stirrer up, and reformer of all things wrong" (Payne, 173), was the great-granddaughter of William Ellery Channing (Transcendentalist and Unitarian minister), had taught Sunday School from the age of seventeen, had been president of her school's graduating class, was an active member of Philadelphia's socially conscious Civic Club, and at twenty-seven was the youngest member of the Philadelphia Board of Education. Darwin Payne makes clear that Molly's civic activism troubled Wister deeply, though he felt uneasy about his objections to it.

In the novel Wister writes: "There's an old maid at home who's charitable, and belongs to the Cruelty to Animals, and she never knows whether she had better cross in front of a street car or wait. I named the hen after her" (51). So it begins. The narrator makes fun of Em'ly because she is huge, gaunt, ugly, and obsessed by an insane sense of responsibility. "Her eye was remarkably bright, but somehow it had an outraged expression. It was as if she went about the world perpetually scandalized over the doings that fell beneath her notice. Her legs were blue, long, and remarkably stout" (51).

The visual pun on "bluestocking" suits perfectly this classic stereotype of the female reformer. And "there is something wrong with her tail." It is phallic. "I think she came near being a rooster," says the Virginian. "She's sure manly-lookin" (51). The narrator, accordingly, finds Em'ly's attempts to mother the offspring of other animals "indiscriminate and reckless," and he punishes her—he calls it "playing a trick"—by giving her stones to sit on. The Virginian, thinking to improve the situation, gives her another chicken's egg to hatch instead. But when the chick emerges long before the usual time, since the egg has already been incubated for three weeks, it drives Em'ly crazy. "Her head lifted nearly off her neck, and in her brilliant yellow eye [there was] an expression of more than outrage at this overturning of a natural law." She screamed all day long, until, in the evening, her voice "had risen . . . several notes into a slim, acute level of terror, and was not like . . . any sound I ever heard before or since. . . . We went in to supper, and I came out to find the hen lying on the ground, dead" (56–57).

After this prank with the hen, the narrator tells us that he and the Virginian "were thorough friends," "all the other barriers between us" having been obliterated. Though it's all supposed to be in good fun, the story of Em'ly, with its spurious air of jocularity, is a vicious attack on the do-good activities of women like Molly Wister who, on this account, have unsexed themselves by going about the world "perpetually scandalized," trying to set things right. Some hatred of the female puts forth its features in this episode, a hatred that seems directly related to feelings of solidarity and intimacy among men. It suggests that the paradise of heterosexual love the novel is headed toward is more of a dream than a reality.

But even more indicative of trouble to come is the treatment of the heroine, Molly Wood. Though the novel seems infatuated with her for about two-thirds of its length, it turns on her without warning near the end, reducing her to a status that is little better than that of Em'ly the hen (who is the heroine in another form). In fact, Molly is society's "happy" version of Em'ly; she is the hen who doesn't refuse the rooster, and so can assume her rightful place in the social order. What that place is becomes clear once Molly has decided to marry the Virginian: "By love and her surrender to him," Wister writes, "their positions had been exchanged" (256). Whereas once he had been her worshipper and she his superior, now the roles are reversed. He is "victorious," and she has given way "before the onset of the natural man himself." "She knew her cowboy lover, with all that he lacked, to be more than ever she could be, with all that she had. He was her worshipper still, but her master, too" (256). The passage shows that what has been at stake all along between Molly and the Virginian is who shall be master, and Wister goes to considerable lengths to show who that is.

The lengths to which he goes suggest that the real target here is not the Virginian's sweetheart or Wister's wife but the truly domineering figure in the author's life, Sarah Wister. Molly's surrender represents not simply the defeat of a female by a male but also the defeat of the genteel tradition—identified with women, religion, and culture—by a rugged man of the outdoors. Molly hails from Bennington, Vermont, where social life is controlled by women— her mother, her sister, her aunt—a matriarchal society that values social position, manners, education, good grammar, the correct accent, and the right clothes, and closely resembles the one Wister inherited from his mother in all but the geographical respect. It is a culture that emasculates men: Molly's brother-in-law is powerless to act against his wife's wishes, and her former suitor, Sam Bannett, is a parody of a sissified, ineffectual male. More than once we are told that in preferring the Virginian, Molly shows she wants "a man who is a man."

The Virginian, on the other hand, belongs to a stronger breed identified with the men of the South and the West, who are uneducated, antireligious, agrarian, and populist. He comes from a Virginia farming family (all boys), has never read a serious book, is "not among those who say their prayers," and subscribes to the author's Darwinian "let the best man win" philosophy. His skills are roping cattle, shooting pistols, riding horses, and bossing hands.

The resemblance between the Virginian's relation to Molly Wood and Wister's relation to his mother when Wister first went west is not an accident. (Nor is the fainter shadowing of the rivalry between Pierce Butler of the Georgia plantations and Fanny Kemble of the London stage.) Wister's mother is a more formidable and extreme version of Molly (who is also a version of Wister's wife). His mother was everything the West was not: society, art, manners, taste, inherited wealth, good breeding, a life of leisure in exquisite surroundings—everything exclusive, discriminating, and genteel. The Virginian's triumph over Molly—their "exchange" of "positions," her "surrender," his becoming "master"—makes sense when one considers Wister's need to be independent of his mother, without losing her regard. Since he had long ago agreed to let her pleasure come out of his life, he cannot openly rebel but must confront her indirectly, in a fiction where finally their positions are reversed.

His mother's presence as a shadow figure behind the heroine of *The Virginian* explains why Wister chose the duel that climaxes the rivalry between the hero and Trampas as the moment to stage Molly's complete and final surrender to the hero ("at the last white-hot edge of ordeal, it was she who renounced and he who had his way"). Wister chose the gunfight between the hero and his enemy as the moment at which to reenact the duel between the hero and the heroine because these conflicts are interdependent. Though usually performed in the name of keeping the woman safe, the gunfight is the antithesis of everything she stands for, engaged in by the hero because he needs to do the unspeakable, needs to break out, needs to feel himself free from the trammels of maternal control. It cannot be fortuitous that the shoot-out is staged time and time again in Westerns as a direct violation of what the woman in the story wants: it is not only Molly in *The Virginian* who says that if her lover goes against Trampas in a gun battle she won't marry him; Amy in *High Noon* says that if her newly wedded husband faces the bandit Frank Miller, she will leave him; Marian Starrett in *Shane* pleads with her husband not to go up against Riker; and scores of other women in scores of other Western movies do the same. The man's reasoning is always that honor demands he meet the challenge, with honor presented as an exigency only he understands. But what honor is is the need to do exactly that which the woman most hates and fears in order to prove that you are not under her control. Moreover, in each case not only does the man do exactly what the woman has begged him not to do, but she takes him back after he has done it. The rejection, in other words, is completely safe. No wonder the Western was popular!

The struggle to be free and independent of his mother was for Wister—as for most men—a life-or-death proposition, more necessary to his survival than the vanquishing of a villain. The shoot-out in *The Virginian* lets us see the incident that climaxes most Westerns not simply as an outpouring of male violence against another male but also as a revolt against the rule of women. It is a moment of rebellion, of escape from the clutches of female authority. Why does the climactic moment in Westerns occur in opposition to a woman's will? Because the meaning of the action *lies* in its opposition to female authority. In the light of Owen Wister's history, *The Virginian* shows more clearly than other Westerns the relationship between actual life and the classic form of the Western story. Westerns are not only in revolt, historically, against a female-dominated culture; they stage a moment in the psychosocial development of the male that requires that he demonstrate his independence from and superiority to women, specifically to his mother. Seen from this perspective, the Western is a gigantic coming-of-age plot in which the hero proves to himself and anyone who will pay attention that he isn't Mama's boy anymore; he is a man.

That is why in *The Virginian* and in every Western since, the concept of being a man looms so large and is reiterated so tirelessly, as if to say "be a man" were the end-all of human utterance. It is no accident that Owen Wister insisted his mother would have hated Wyoming, and felt he was reborn there, and based his reputation in the world on his Western experiences. Wister did in Wyoming what every young man wants to do—proved he could be strong and independent. And that is why *The Virginian* caught on. Wister gave a local habitation and a name, a way of dressing, moving, talking, and behaving to the stage of life that represents a break from maternal control. He acted out on a stage that was thrillingly stark and exotic a drama in which every man could share.

Wister's relation to his mother reveals that the desire for domination that characterizes the hero's relation to practically everything—the land, animals, women, men, his own body—can be seen as re-active, less an outlet for aggression than a response to his fear of not having a separate existence. The need for an outward display of strength and independence on the hero's part is so strong an element in Westerns that it controls virtually every aspect of the genre, especially the hero's relation to other human beings. He shows his independence through the successful domination of other men. This superior status is won through the hero's actual perfor-mance only secondarily; in the final analysis, it is his birthright. His mastery is projected backward to the moment of conception and beyond; for the hero belongs to a race of heroes, which is to say, he belongs to the dominant race.

In an essay published seven years before *The Virginian*, called "The Evolution of the Cow-Puncher," Wister argued that the cow-boy is a lineal descendant of the Anglo-Saxon knight-at-arms, a man in whom the rugged outdoor life of the West has brought out the latent courage, heroism, and toughness of his kind. For Wister, clearly, the attributes of heroic manhood—courage, toughness—are closely bound up with race.

Anglo-Saxon blood makes every cowboy a natural aristocrat. "In personal daring and in skill as to the horse, the knight and the cowboy are nothing but the same Saxon of different environments" (606). As proof of his racial theory, Wister tells, with great relish, the story of an English nobleman who came to Texas and was transformed into a cowboy almost overnight: "The man's outcome typifies the way of his race from the beginning. Hundreds like him have gone to Australia, Canada, India, and have done likewise, and in our own continent you may see the thing plainer than anywhere else" (603). The Englishman turned cowboy is the archetypal colonial conqueror, adapting himself to the immediate conditions, subduing the environment to his will.

Wister's identification of the cowpuncher with the Anglo-Saxon knight-at-arms is a way for an upper-class composer-turned-short-story-writer with doubts about his independence to claim a robust masculinity. For if an English nobleman can become an overnight cowboy, why not a genteel fellow from Philadelphia? (The cowboy self was there all along; the West has only brought it out in him.) The racism is a move toward self-definition that emphasizes manliness above all other qualities and confers the right to lordship over other human beings.

Wister's racism, if not his cowboy self, predated his entry into adulthood; he inherited it, along with the family estates. The origins of his social attitudes are illustrated in a passage from the diary of Sidney George Fisher, a longtime friend of his mother with a deep interest in the family. Owen Wister is referred to in this excerpt by his nickname, "Dan."

Dr. Wister here in the morning. . . . He had his little son they call Dan with him, a remarkably bright, intelligent boy. Dan, some weeks ago, went with his mother to pay a visit to her father at his plantation in Georgia. Before she went, Dan's father told him that the Negroes would not call him Massa now, but Bub, at which Dan was very indignant. The morning after they arrived at Savannah, Dan went out into the entry, where two clean, well dressed Negro women met him & immediately exclaimed "Oh what a nice young Massa, good morning young Massa." "That is the way," said Dan, "in which I always expect to be addressed." Recollecting this, I said to him this morning, "Well, Dan, I suppose you saw plenty of Negroes at the plantation." "Yes indeed." "And how did they treat you? Very politely I suppose." "They treated me very kindly," said Dan, with emphasis. I have no doubt they did, for they are old family Negroes who have come back to work for Butler & are said to work very well. (quoted in Bell, 400–401)

The childhood anecdote suggests how his family circumstances formed Wister's attitudes toward race and indicates how natural it would have been for him to have adopted a white supremacist point of view as part of his concept of heroism. His second novel, *Lady Baltimore* (1906), even makes white racial superiority one of its explicit themes. But the notion of race was important to Wister's construction of the Western hero (and of himself) in *The Virginian* as well, and it has played a significant role in the racial politics of the genre ever since.

Wister's Anglo-Saxon chauvinism is not spelled out in capital letters in *The Virginian*, but it crops up almost immediately in an early scene where the hero has just met four drummers (salesmen) described by his friend, Steve, as "two Jews handling cigars, one American with consumption-killer, and a Dutchman with jew'lry." Steve adds: "the American looks like he washed the oftenest" (20). One of the Jews insists that he and the Virginian have met before in Chicago at a place called Ikey's. Such familiarity is offensive and vulgar to the cowboy from Virginia, and to show his contempt for the man's lack of refinement, the Virginian delivers a clever insult, mastering the situation. The hero's mastery depends on our assuming a standard of behavior that is derived from Philadelphia and Newport—from the Anglo-Saxon gentry—and not from any universal or God-given social code. The Virginian's victories on the field of manners naturalize his particular code, make it seem the universal form of fine behavior, while the victories themselves are made possible in the eyes of the reading audience by the cultural dominance of the class, race, and ethnic group Wister belonged to.

For example, in a climactic episode, the Virginian humiliates his men in front of a crowd of wealthy Easterners by suckering them with a tall tale. The trick depends on their ignorance of fancy restaurants and Eastern high life, and upon his knowledge of these things. But the conclusion we are supposed to draw is that the Virginian is *innately* superior; he comes out on top not because he has been socialized by his family background or has consciously learned the right rules but because he was born to win. In social situations, as in the event of an Indian attack, he just knows what's right.

The Western hero who seems to come from nowhere in fact belongs to the dominant race and class. He stands as a bulwark, a fortress against dangers from without and from within. He cannot come in a variety of shapes and colors but must always exhibit the same set of attributes—those of the power elite—because his social function, among other things, was to ensure that the kinds of people who are in power will remain there. Fear of change in the form of contamination by inferior breeds is as much a part of the Western's racism as is its assertion of Anglo-Saxon superiority. That is why in Westerns that succeed *The Virginian* a Mexican is almost never the leading man, the whole point being to maintain the hierarchy that exists in the society the Western plays to.

In his essay on the cowpuncher Wister portrayed the American continent as threatened by "debased and mongrel . . . hordes of encroaching alien vermin, that turn our cities to Babels and our citizenship to a hybrid farce, who degrade our commonwealth from a nation into something half pawn-shop, half broker's office" (207). Wister's use of words like *mongrel* and *hybrid* to describe immigrant populations suggests a fear of mixing with others that sounds like his socially conservative mother, with her horror of associating with all kinds of people. For while he gloried in the experience of rubbing elbows with disreputable types, Wister's attitudes replicated his mother's, as well as those of a large sector of the population at the time. He writes just after a huge wave of immigration had activated fears in the WASP establishment of contamination and takeover by "darker" races, chiefly Jews and eastern Europeans. It was also the era when, in the wake of Reconstruction, antiblack sentiment was running strong. But Wister's racism has a psychological as well as a political aspect.

I've said that the child inside the Western hero could be equated with his animal self, spontaneous and unreconstructed, and that while Westerns appeal to a desire for an unhampered life in the flesh, they also require that such desires be renounced or indefinitely postponed. The presence of women evokes and is identified with the child self in the hero: as maternal figures, women remind him of his vulnerability and dependence; and as objects of sexual desire, they remind him of the desires of his flesh. To be adult and to survive in the world the Western posits means to assert dominance over the tremulous, fleshly, mortal part of the self.

In *The Virginian* as in many Westerns, the child self is identified not only with women—Molly Wood/Sarah Wister—but also with socially unacceptable others: people who don't know the rules (like the Jew who talked too much), or who don't play by them (like Trampas and his cattle-stealing friends), or who haven't got any social or economic power (like the hands the Virginian is in charge of). Thus, the Huns and the Poles line up with an array of figures and forces that must be conquered or extirpated if the hero is to prevail, some of which form part of the social world the hero inhabits, and some of which exist inside himself, as emotional alternatives to his mode of life. These forces, outside and in, are not necessarily distinct. When the cowhands bellow out their rebellious song, "I'm wild and woolly and full of fleas," you can bet that a part of Wister wishes he could be, too. The alien vermin would not be despised with such energy if they did not represent something Wister felt stirring within himself.

It is this inner domain that finally betrays him.

One of the most appealing aspects of *The Virginian* is the extent to which it seems willing to count the cost of being a hero. More than most Westerns, the novel offers glimpses into the interior where the price of heroism is paid, glimpses that let us see that the Virginian's lazy, effortless control of all situations is not the whole story, and which reveal shapes and longings that have no counterpart in anything we have been explicitly told.

Several of these glimpses involve the Virginian's feelings for his friend Steve, an elusive though pivotal presence in the novel. Steve is the occasion for the first genuine outburst of emotion on the hero's part, an outburst that occurs when he is out of his mind, and which indicates a life going on in the depths of his being that never shows itself on the surface.

> "Steve!" the sick man now cried out, in poignant appeal.
> "Steve!" To the women it was a name unknown—unknown as was also this deep inward tide of feeling which he could no longer conceal, being himself no longer. (195)

The "deep inward tide of feeling" belongs to a subterranean level of the hero's psyche which can only be caught sight of when he is not himself. Especially since the object of this feeling is not Molly Stark Wood but the "rollicking man," Steve, the Virginian's best friend, whose "tiger undulation of form" so caught the narrator's eye on first meeting. To the women "it is a name unknown," since the love adult males feel for one another can receive no outward expression in the society Wister and his characters inhabit. But the Virginian's love for Steve and the narrator's love for the Virginian are strands of feeling that run throughout the story, though they are never named.

The Virginian's relation to Steve is the most charged relationship in the novel (the narrator's relation to the Virginian is a mirror image of it); it is also the least available to inspection. Steve is the only person who calls the protagonist by a proper name, "Jeff," which signals an intimacy attained by no other character. And though the Virginian says after Steve's hanging, "I knew Steve awful well," we know practically nothing of him. One now and then gets the feeling that if times had been different this could have been a story about "Jeff" and Steve, instead of a story about the character we know as the Virginian and Molly Stark Wood.

The sudden opening of a chasm of feeling inside the hero with the cry "Steve!" takes the women by surprise, but it should not surprise us. Steve is the person Wister might have loved if he had stayed in Europe and studied music, or stayed on in Wyoming and gotten to know himself. *The Virginian* is resonant with feelings that attach to these lost possibilities, and much of the power of Wister's descriptions of landscape and cowboys derives from this overwhelming nostalgia. The novel is thick with an air of might-have-been. And of this might-have-been Steve is the chief representative.

The death of Steve is the price the hero pays for becoming successful, being foreman, getting money for a ranch, acquiring authority. His own legitimation and Steve's death are inseparable. Everything Steve stands for is forbidden—same-sex love, breaking the laws of property, being physical and devil-may-care—so in killing Steve, Wister is stamping out something in himself. Not a desire to steal or to have sex with other men, necessarily, but the courage to transgress, whatever form it might take. The Virginian's betrayal of his friend recalls Wister's own self-betrayal when his life was at a crossroads and he obeyed his father instead of himself. So when the Virginian obeys *his* boss, too, and catches and hangs the men who were stealing Judge Henry's cattle, it is consistent.

The sacrifice of the child self is not only a renunciation of certain actions; it means giving up the right to express certain emotions as well. In writing *The Virginian* Wister had the opportunity to express feelings he had no outlet for elsewhere. We have seen how he does this in the chapter on the hen named Em'ly where he vented his anger against civic-minded women. In the chapter about the child-like cowboy, Shorty, and his beloved horse, Pedro, he uses a character to express feelings he cannot exhibit with propriety himself.

When the dim-witted, gullible Shorty has to sell his dearest friend, Pedro, to a man well known for mistreating horses, he hugs the pony good-bye and heads for the ranch house. But before he gets to the pasture bars, he turns around and comes back. He puts his arms around the horse's neck and weeps: "'Good-by, my little horse, my dear horse, my little, little Pedro,' he said as his tears wet the pony's neck. Then he wiped them with his hand and got himself back to the bunkhouse. After breakfast he and his belongings departed to Drybone. . . . The pony stopped feeding to look at the mail-wagon pass by; but the master forbore to turn his head" (173). The tears Shorty cries, his feelings for his horse, are forbidden in the world Wister and the Virginian inhabit, the world we inhabit, and have to be projected onto others. The hero is allowed to beat Shorty's torturer to a pulp, but crying over a horse is something else.

Like Em'ly, Shorty and Pedro are not integral to the external plot, but they are necessary for the emotional logic of the story. Shorty, soon to be killed by Trampas, and Pedro, soon to be beaten, mutilated, and shot, are the animal-child, the cow-boy the Western appeals to in its audience. They are the ones who must be sacrificed in the name of manhood and responsibility. Yet though they must be killed—the code demands it—their deaths must also be avenged. Their persecutors evoke the hero's most vengeful retaliations: in a rage, he beats the man who tortured Pedro, and he kills Shorty's murderer, the villain Trampas.

Shorty and Pedro embody the hero's innocence and vulnerability in a displaced form; killed in that guise, they turn up again. Later in the novel, when the Virginian and the narrator are alone, the child within appears in person, awakened this time by the death of Steve. What upsets the hero more than anything, he says, is not that he has had to hang his best friend but that Steve, at the end, wouldn't speak to him. "He told goodby to the rest of the boys but not to me."

Reminiscing about the years he spent with Steve, and how Steve had then gone his own way, and how when they were about to hang him he had maintained silence, the Virginian breaks down and cries.

He gave a sob. It was the first I had ever heard from him, and before I knew what I was doing I had reined my horse up to his and put my arm around his shoulders. I had no sooner touched him than he was utterly overcome. (229)

This is the only Western novel I have read in which the hero cries, though it is not the only one in which he kills the man he loves. Still haunted by the thought of Steve's death, dreaming about him at night, afraid of his ghost, the Virginian says to the narrator:

I expect in many growed-up men you'd call sensible there's a little boy sleepin'—the little kid they once was—that still keeps his fear of the dark. Well, this experience has woke up that kid in me, and blamed if I can coax the little cuss to go to sleep again! I keep a-telling him daylight will sure come but he keeps a-crying and holding on to me. (239)

It's seldom that Westerns allow the audience to see the child inside the hero, much less call it by name. The entire genre is dedicated to eliminating any hint of its presence, offering a front—tough squint, leathery impassivity—that denies the existence of any such inward reality. But Wister, like Grey, is so close to the nineteenth century that the expression of sentiment has not yet been outlawed completely. Although his business in the novel is to promote the worship of masculine aplomb, he has not yet forgotten that part of himself that is best represented by a frightened child. The Western genre represents an implicit conflict between the child's desire for comfort, love, protection, and satisfaction of its physical and emotional needs and the heroic imperative to be independent, strong, impervious to pain, a silent endurer of suffering. Normally the Western allows only latter alternative to the hero, but Wister's novel lets us at least catch glimpses of the former. As soon as it does, though, the lid goes right back on. When the narrator and Virginian come upon the body of Shorty, who has been killed and left to rot on the trail, they find an old newspaper that Steve had given to Shorty just before he was hung. On it is a note for the Virginian: "I could not have spoke to you without playing the baby." Steve's message both reveals his humanness—his child self—and underlines the importance of keeping it concealed from the world. Rather than risk losing control of himself, Steve, a true man who dies with perfect bearing, hides his feelings from his best friend. Anything is better than playing the baby. Anything is better than losing control, showing weakness, spilling tears, undoing the body's boundaries and exposing one's insides to the world. These possibilities, not ghosts, not death itself, are what the Western hero fears the most.

And most desires. Because he must police his body's boundaries so severely, because he is forbidden to play the baby, because it is better for him to die with his love unspoken than to lose his composure, the pressure the hero feels to dispense with social codes and burst the boundaries all at once is tremendous. One way to do it is to get killed—the body punctured by bullets, face in the dirt, blood mingling with the dust. Another way is imagined by the Virginian at the very end of the novel in a passage I've referred to briefly elsewhere. The Virginian delivers a long soliloquy to Molly—they are far from human habitations—that completely undercuts the model of heroism the novel has been celebrating thus far. They are on an island in a mountain stream:

> Presently, while they remained without speaking by the pool, came a little wild animal swimming round the rock from above. It had not seen them, nor suspected their presence. They held themselves still, watching its alert head cross through the waves quickly and come down through the pool, and so swim to the other side. There it came out on a small stretch of sand, turned its gray head and its pointed black nose this way and that, never seeing them, and then rolled upon its back in the warm dry sand. After a minute of rolling, it got on its feet again, shook its fur, and trotted away.
>
> Then the bridegroom husband opened his shy heart deep down.
>
> "I am like that fellow," he said dreamily. "I have often done the same." . . . "If I could talk his animal language I could talk to him," he pursued. "And he would say to me: 'Come and roll on the sands. Where's the use of fretting? What's the gain in being a man? Come roll on the sands with me.' That's what he would say." The Virginian

paused and went on, always dreamily. "Often when I have come here, it has made me want to become the ground, become the water, become the trees, mix with the whole thing. Not know myself from it. Never unmix again. . . . " (280)

One could not wish for a more eloquent denial of everything this novel has been at pains to promote. The desire for separation from and control of others—hired hands, Jewish drummers, cackling women, cowards. The celebration of competition, conquest, rising in the world, a stiff upper lip, and heterosexual romance. Against all of this the deepest desire of the Western hero is to "mix with the whole thing" and "never unmix again." The child returns one final time as the playful, amphibious "fellow," rolling in the sand, not fretting about anything. After the deaths of Shorty and Pedro, after the deaths of Steve and Trampas, after Molly has been mastered, the hired hands hornswoggled, and the Virginian promoted to foreman with better things in store, it turns out that what he really wants is not any of these things but union with the natural world. An earthy mother.

What makes *The Virginian* so interesting from the standpoint of the history of the Western is that it states so openly the counterargument to its own point of view. Having successfully done everything society and his own instincts suggested—leaving his mother and proving his ability to compete in a man's world—and having won both games and been given everything he wanted—a girl, victory over his enemies, a ranch waiting in the future—Wister's hero is ready to chuck it all. On his honeymoon, he asks, "What's the gain in being a man?" and says he'd rather be a little wild animal swimming in a pool, he'd rather be earth . . . water . . . trees . . .

Photograph of Zane Grey at Betatakin.
Courtesy of Loren Grey.

Zane Grey ☆
Writing the Purple Sage

8

Riders of the Purple Sage (1912) is not like *The Virginian*. Zane Grey didn't come from an upper-class background; no one in his family knew Henry James; and his prose doesn't sound like he's been reading Thackeray and Austen. It's wonderful writing, but not in good taste. For sheer emotional force; for the capacity to get and keep his readers, absolutely, in his grip; for the power to be—there is no other word for it—thrilling, few practitioners of narrative prose can equal Grey. Sometimes reading him is like being caught in a waterfall or a flood; you feel at the mercy of a natural force that cannot be emanating entirely from the page.

The world in Grey's novels is and isn't the same one Owen Wister represents. It's the West, cowboys, outlaws, romance, death, and shooting. But the inflection, the tincture, the medium of refraction differ. For purposes of comparison, one might say *The Virginian* is a novel of manners set in Wyoming, while *Riders of the Purple Sage* is a novel of passion, where passion runs equally in the watercourses of Utah and in the blood of the hero and heroine. It's not that the issues these writers address are so different: they both feel some principle of vitality in the landscape that transforms everything; both strive to make some authentic connection to that life. But where Wister tries to do it in the form of a stage play with Western props,

Grey's canvas is the cosmos, and anything can be pigment: blood, wind, buttes, bullets, tears.

Grey's full name was Pearl Zane Gray. People called him "Pearl" while he was growing up (Pearl wasn't that uncommon a name for a man in those days), but later on, when he overheard two young women on a train discussing his work and one of them referred to him as "she," he dropped it; he also changed the spelling of his last name from Gray to Grey. His other name, Zane, came to him from his great-great-grandfather, Colonel Ebenezer Zane, who founded Zanesville, Ohio, where Grey grew up. This famous ancestor had held Fort Henry against the Indians for twenty years, and his sister, Elizabeth Zane, had risked her life by running the gauntlet of Indian gunfire to carry powder to the fort. "When I read it in the Fourth Reader," Grey wrote, "I thrilled with pride."

Everything in Grey's life suggests that he wanted to be a hero on the ancestral model. He saw his life in the image of theirs and of the dime novel heroes he worshipped as a child. According to his biographer, Frank Gruber, whenever Grey got into a fistfight, it wasn't just because he was mad; it would be on behalf of a younger brother hit by a baseball bat, or because some mean boys were throwing stones at an old man. His childhood, as Gruber presents it, and as Grey himself writes about it in an article on his early career, was a tissue of images drawn from the boy's adventure stories that he feasted on.

"I belonged to a gang of young ruffians, or, rather, youthful desperadoes who were bound to secrecy by oaths and the letting of blood," Grey wrote in an article on his early career. "We had a complete collection of Beadle's Dime Library and some of Harry Castleman's books, the reading of which could be earned only by a deed of valor" ("Breaking Through," 13). Having read about gangs and caves in Deadwood Dick, Grey organized a gang that dug a cave where he and his friends could hole up to read more stories about gangs and caves. Then Grey, in the cave, wrote a story called "Jim of the Cave," which "had to do with a gang of misunderstood boys, a girl with light hair and blue eyes; dark nights, secrets, fight, blood, and sudden death." The identities and parallels here among what Grey reads, what he does, and what he writes continue throughout his life.

Grey won a baseball scholarship to the University of Pennsylvania because of having pitched a no-hitter in Baltimore, Ohio, where he barely escaped being tarred and feathered and run out of town on a rail for throwing curve balls. In his last year at college he came up to bat in the ninth inning with two men out and one on second— Penn was playing the University of Virginia, having beaten Cornell, Johns Hopkins, Lehigh, Harvard, and even—in an exhibition game—the New York Giants:

> As Pearl came to bat, a professor shouted, "Gray, the honor of the University of Pennsylvania rests with you!" Pearl hit a home run and won the game. The crowd covered him with roses, and the papers called him the real-life Frank Merriwell, the popular fiction character who always came up to bat in the last half of the ninth and won the game. (Gruber, 14)

Grey *was* the real-life Frank Merriwell. He had graduated from the escapades of Deadwood Dick to those of the college hero. Soon the model for heroic action would shift again.

After studying dentistry at the University of Pennsylvania (his father had been a dentist), Grey went to New York and hung out a shingle. A relative of a friend of my family actually had her teeth fixed by Zane Grey, and according to legend he didn't do such a great job. But being a great dentist was not his aim. His aim was to write. He had gone to New York because it was the center of the publishing world, and dentistry was only a way to put food on the table. From now on the story would no longer be about Deadwood Dick or Frank Merriwell; its subject would be the artist as romantic hero.

The terms Grey uses to describe his struggles as an author are hyperbolic, and it is tempting to make fun of him for it. When he left New York to devote himself to writing full-time, as he tells it, he was "crossing the Rubicon" and pitting his "puny strength" against "mountainous obstacles." But the facts of the case bear him out. In 1902, after several publishers had turned it down, his wife-to-be, Lina Elise Roth (known as Dolly), financed the publication of his first novel, *Betty Zane*, which he'd slaved over, a book about the famous ancestor who had carried gunpowder to the fort. Saving the fort was the role Dolly would play in Grey's life from that time on. She taught him the grammar, spelling, and punctuation he hadn't bothered to learn in school; copied his manuscripts for him in longhand; and, most important, gave his work constant and unstinting praise. When his next two novels had to be given away for practically nothing and Grey was ready to quit, Dolly urged him to keep on. After five years of grueling effort, all Grey had to show was a mass of rejection slips; he was borrowing money from his brother and living off his wife's inheritance, having long since used up his savings.

Then something happens that could only have happened to Grey. He went to a lecture at the Campfire Club in New York, given by a character named Colonel Buffalo Jones. Jones was trying to raise money to breed a new kind of animal called the cattalo—half buffalo, half cow—as part of an effort to save the buffalo from extinction. But no one believed the incredible stories he told about his experiences hunting buffalo and other animals, because the audience had no knowledge of the West. They hooted him down. Afterward Grey sought Buffalo Jones out in his hotel room and found him sick and low on cash. He took care of him for a couple of days and convinced him that what he needed was someone to go on a hunting expedition with him who could write a book that would prove his stories were true. He proposed himself for the job, and Jones accepted. The only trouble was, Grey would have to pay his own way, and given the state of his finances that meant he couldn't go. But Dolly insisted; she felt this trip would be the making of him and used the last of her inheritance to finance it. Grey went, had a "magnificent adventure," met the man (Jim Emmett) on whom most of his heroes would be based, and absorbed the materials that made him famous for the rest of his life.

But the "terrible ordeal" phase was not over yet. Grey put everything he had quite literally into his book about Buffalo Jones, *The Last of the Plainsmen*. An editor at Harper's had expressed an interest in the project, so Grey had high hopes that this time he would succeed. A few weeks after he handed in the manuscript, the editor wrote asking him to come to New York. Grey took the train with great anticipation and was greeted with words he never forgot: "I don't see anything in this to convince me you can write either narrative or fiction":

> I was stunned. I could not speak a word. Taking the manuscript, I went out. A terrible commotion labored in my breast. When I reached the wide staircase my eyes began to grow dim, my mouth went dry, and my body became cold as ice.
>
> When I reached the corner of Pearl Street, I leaned against a tall iron post. There my sight failed me entirely. I clutched the post with one arm and the manuscript with the other. That was the most exceedingly bitter moment of my life.

For most people that would have been the climax of the incident and the end of a career. But not for Grey.

> Suddenly something marvelous happened to me, in my mind, to my eyesight, to my breast. That moment should logically have been the end of my literary aspirations! From every point of view I seemed lost. But someone inside me cried out: "*He* does not know! *They* are all wrong!" ("Breaking Through," 11–12)

This extraordinary phenomenon is typical of Grey's life and work. Things become animate that had simply been objects, and the self, suddenly dispersed, is inhabited by alien forces. "From every point of view I seemed lost" is not just a metaphor; the "I" has literally disappeared momentarily. The fracturing of consciousness, sense of possession, sudden animation of the surroundings, and abrupt switch from one mental state to another are an animating principle of his fiction. And so is the strange doubling that occurs here: his conversion experience happens not just anywhere but on Pearl Street. It's as if the driving force of the emotion being experienced had momentarily pushed through whatever it is that separates consciousness from its surroundings, bodies from other bodies. The volcanic energy of his feelings produces a moment of transport in which Grey is carried out of himself to the point where there *is* no difference between him and the world around. Such moments distill the essence of Grey's life and work. It doesn't matter whether the transport occurs while he is reading *Frank in the Mountains*, or writing about Frank in the mountains, or being Frank in the mountains. What matters is, he has been transported.

Here is another example of what I mean. Grey's biographer, Frank Gruber, opens his life of Grey with a picture of a boy on a country road waiting impatiently for the next issue of *Michigan Farmer*, which has just begun publishing a serial by Grey called *The Light of Western Stars*.

> I read the first installment and was enthralled. I could scarcely wait for the following Tuesday, when the mailman delivered the new issue, and in the succeeding weeks I would be out on the road an hour before the expected arrival of the R.F.D. mail carrier. I would snatch the mail from his hand and for the next fifteen or twenty minutes I would be lost to the world. (vii)

The child who passionately craves the next installment—Gruber himself, of course—grows up to become a well-known author of Western novels and screenplays, and goes on to write a biography of Grey which sounds just like the adventure stories both of them read and wrote.

I am not talking about literary influence here; or rather, I am talking about what literary influence *really* is. When Grey hits a home run, or spends his wife's last nickel on a trip to see a man who wrestles mountain lions with his bare hands, that is literary influence. It comes from reading *Frank in the Mountains* and *Frank at Don Carlos' Ranch*. It comes from reading about ancestors who saved the fort in the Fourth Reader. When that other Frank, Frank Gruber, lifts his eyes from the pages of *The Light of Western Stars* and leaves his Michigan roadside to become a writer of Westerns and a biographer of Grey, that, too, is literary influence: pure emulation of an admired model. The light of the western stars, we might say, shines directly into Frank Gruber's soul and creates him in the image Grey created, which was created in turn by his ancestors and his reading, and so on. Filiation, in the history of the Western, doesn't distinguish between texts and persons. Literature and heroic living are one and the same.

If you don't believe me, listen to the life of that other son of the sagebrush, Louis L'Amour, whose biographical sketch appears at the back of the more than one hundred million volumes he has in print.

> As a boy growing up in North Dakota, he absorbed all he could about his family's frontier heritage, including the story of his great-grandfather who was scalped by Sioux warriors. . . . Mr. L'Amour left home at the age of fifteen and enjoyed a wide variety of jobs including seaman, lumberjack, elephant handler, skinner of dead cattle, assessment miner, and officer on tank destroyers during World War II. . . . He also circled the world on a freighter, sailed a dhow on the Red Sea, was shipwrecked in the West Indies and stranded in the Mojave Desert. He has won fifty-one of fifty-nine fights as a professional boxer and worked as a journalist and lecturer.

L'Amour, one of the four most popular authors in the world today, wrote four hundred short stories and more than eighty-five novels, an accomplishment that, in the tradition I am describing, is perfectly continuous with prize fighting and dhow sailing. Reading, writing, and living dangerously in this tradition are not qualitatively different ways of being in the world but are simply transformations of a single set toward experience.

After the incident on Pearl Street, Grey's life changed drastically. He went home to Pennsylvania, got to work on a novel which was accepted by Harper's (*Heritage of the Desert*, 1910), and then wrote *Riders of the Purple Sage*, the most famous of all Western novels. Grey's novels made the best-seller list nine times between 1914 and 1928, a figure not matched by any other writer in the first half of the twentieth century. His books continued to sell well until his death in 1939, and more movies were made from them than from those of any other author. In his lifetime he wrote sixty novels, fifty-six of them Westerns, as well as several novels for young people, books and magazine pieces on fishing and hunting, and dozens of short stories. One biographer estimates that he wrote an average of a hundred thousand words a year, not counting the five or six long, involved letters he wrote every day.

For Grey as for L'Amour, writing was a matter not just of *representing* deeds of valor but of performing them. Unlike Max Brand, who wrote about the West from an apartment in Florence where he went to study Italian art, Grey did not churn the novels out while his real interests lay elsewhere; he sweated them, one by one. Being, acting, and writing formed a perfect continuum: as you were, so would you write. Since his own idea of greatness was modeled on the heroes of adventure stories, he describes the writer as a kind of gallant explorer, who "looks at things so keenly as to find unknown characteristics, unsuspected points of view, secret depths, the life & soul of natural facts." "Every situation" must "yield significance for thought." Above all, he believed, "a writer must have strong and noble convictions about life." Grey translated the physical ruggedness and capacity to stand pain he required of his adventurer heroes into a kind of military discipline he required of himself as craftsman. He devoured manuals of composition and devised rules for himself which he cast in the form of muscular aphorisms and parade ground commands: "Eternal vigilance is the price of a good style." "Brevity helps action and makes strength and force." "Do not crowd in irrelevant thoughts." "Do not change subject if it can be helped." "Cut out intensive expression and superlatives." "Do not use second person" (quoted in Carlton Jackson, 119–20).

As the attempt to impose martial self-discipline implies, the ordeal phase, for Grey, was never really over. His diaries record agonizing struggles to produce, superhuman effort, self-flagellation, exhaustion, exhilaration, triumph, and release. While composing *Wanderer of the Wasteland* (1923), the novel he hoped would make his reputation as a serious writer, Grey experienced drastic changes of mood on a daily and even hourly basis.

> A hyena lying in ambush—that is my black spell!—I conquered one mood only to fall prey to the next. And there have been days of hell. Hopeless, black, morbid, sickening, exaggerated, mental disorder! I know my peril—that I must rise out of it, very soon for good and all, or surrender forever. It took a day—a whole endless day of crouching in a chair, hating self and all, the sunshine, the sound of laughter, and then I wandered about like a lost soul, or a man who was conscious of imminent death. And I ached all over, my eyes blurred, my head throbbed, and there was pain in my heart. Today I began to mend and now there is hope. (quoted in Carlton Jackson, *Zane Grey*, 143)

Six months later he would write: "I believe absolutely in myself, my singular place, my gifts, my force.... My zeal to work, my destiny...." Conrad's Kurtz could not have said it better.

Wanderer of the Wasteland concerns a man who lives a life of exile in the desert in a bitter effort to regain his soul. Throughout his life, Grey explored the deserts and mountains of the West compulsively on expeditions which he alternated with deep-sea fishing trips. These trips were not merely recreational, they kept him alive in every sense: psychically, physically, creatively. Grey tried to explain to himself why this was so in an essay called "What the Desert Means to Me."

Grey's relationship to the physical environment was as deep and intense as any relationship can be. When he writes "that wild, lonely, purple land of sage and rock took possession of me," the metaphor of possession can be taken literally. He describes the desert as a seducer who tempts him with death.

> The lure of the silent waste places of the earth, how inexplicable and tremendous! Why do men sacrifice love, home, civilization for the solitude of the lonely land? How infinite the fascination of death and decay and desolation—the secret of the desert! ("What the Desert Means to Me," 5)

Grey found it necessary to be alone as much as possible in the wild: "The lonely places seemed to be mine, and I was jealous of them. Always I was watching and listening." He developed the habit on camping trips of going off by himself to some hill or clump of cedars, "there to listen and to watch. This seemed to me to be a communion with the strange affinity of the desert." Gradually, as he tries to understand why these experiences filled him with vague happiness, his vocabulary shifts away from images of possession and seduction and becomes more tranquil and detached:

> It became an imperative thing for me to find out what took place in my mind during these idle, dreaming hours. The mystery augmented with the discovery that at such moments and hours I did nothing— nothing but gaze over the desolate desert, over the beautiful purple-sage uplands, listening to the wind in the cedars, the rustling sand along the rock, the scream of an eagle or cry of a lonely bird. I hardly knew I was there. (6)

As he starts to be able to produce this "lost to the world" experience voluntarily, he comes to believe that "the fleeting trances belonged to the savage past. I was a savage. I could bring back for a brief instant the sensory state of the progenitors of the human race." Grey interpreted his experience in the terms evolutionary theory had made available, talking about the red blood of the ancestors that runs in every man and woman and "the ineradicable and unconscious wild-

ness of savage nature in them." But at the same time Grey declares
that all his writing is addressed to the savage part of men, he speaks
proudly of human evolution beyond the primitive, and seems to embrace an ideology of progress, imagining the primitive both as something to be transcended *and* as transcendence itself:

> Harness the cave-man—yes! as Doctor Fosdick so eloquently preaches;
> but do not kill him. Something of the wild and primitive should forever
> remain instinctive in the human race. All the joy of the senses lives in
> this law. The sweetness of the childhood of the race comes back in this
> thoughtless watching and listening. Perhaps the spirit of this marvellous
> nature is in reality God. (7)

In the course of this paragraph God and the caveman are con-
flated, an intellectual contradiction that reflects an emotional truth
central to Grey's work. Novel after novel dramatizes an interplay of
forces whose value and identity are always shifting: cosmic, psychic,
demonic, divine—they sweep through the life-world of his fiction
upsetting the normal relations of things in vertiginous moments that
replay the Pearl Street incident over and over again. The desert
landscape, alternately heaven or hell, is the place where this metaphysical vertigo manifests itself. Landscape, the site of transport,
plays everything out in its own body: emotion, action, identity,
history, fate, and dream.

In *Riders of the Purple Sage* the natural setting steals the show so
continually from the characters that it almost doesn't make sense
to speak of it as a setting. The names Grey gives to places—Surprise
Valley, Deception Pass—change them from backdrops against
which events take place into events themselves. Even the coloration
of the landscape activates it. The purple sage, the yellow dust, the
amber spring, the silver aspens, the heroine's horses "Black Star"
and "Night," her herds—referred to as the "red herd" and the "white

herd"—function as animate elements of design. They wheel and turn in the plot and express thoughts and feelings in exactly the same way the characters do: in Grey, you never know what nature will do next. But in treating landscape this way, it is not as though Grey were trying to work through a philosophical problem that we would describe perhaps as the relation of subject to object. Grey's dramas of psyche and landscape do not translate readily into the vocabularies that philosophy and psychology provide.

The following experience, for example, happens to a man named Venters:

> Above him, through the V-shaped cleft in the dark rim of the cliff, shone the lustrous stars that had been his lonely accusers for a long, long year. To-night they were different. He studied them. Larger, whiter, more radiant they seemed; but that was not the difference he meant. Gradually it came to him that the distinction was not one he saw, but one he felt. In this he divined as much of the baffling change as he thought would be revealed to him then. And as he lay there, with the singing of the cliff-winds in his ears, the white stars above the dark, bold vent, the difference which he felt was that he was no longer alone. (91)

This incident is a complicated transposition of the epiphany on the corner of Pearl Street. Then Grey stood at a crossroads in his life and the world took on his name. This time a man named Venters registers the change that has taken place in his life by looking at a world that mirrors his name. Venters sees the stars through a "V-shaped cleft," a "dark, bold vent," and, as if this were not enough, at the moment when he feels himself no longer alone, he hears "cliff-winds singing in his ears"—the root meaning of *vent* being "wind." These verbal coincidences seem to show Venters *literally*, through letters, not just that he is no longer alone but that in some sense he *is* the world he beholds.

At moments like these, the boundaries between self and world are completely redrawn. Identity isn't so much lost or dispersed, as in the Pearl Street example, as it is redistributed across boundaries.

The cliff and the man are no longer different *kinds* of things but possess a common nature; they are, for an instant, twins. One doesn't know whether Grey was aware of what he was doing here or not, but this question, which keeps on surfacing as one reads, is really superfluous in the end. It becomes apparent that *our* questions about what Grey was doing stem from assumptions about the relation between conscious and unconscious knowledge that passages like this one, with their radical reapportionment of mind, self, and body, simply abrogate. Though we may need to translate such moments into a more systematized and abstract idiom in order to understand them, we must realize that ours are not the master tropes, and that talk of identity and boundaries, consciousness and its objects, over-determination and intertextuality, tends not only to flatten and oversimplify but also to misconstrue and distort what Grey is representing. Here is another example of what I mean (this is Venters again):

> Then the huge, notched bulge of the red rim loomed over him, a mark by which he knew again the deep cove where his camp lay hidden. As he penetrated the thicket, safe again for the present, his thoughts reverted to the girl he had left there. . . . The girl lay with wide-open, dark eyes, and they dilated when he knelt beside her. (55–56)

What draws our attention here, at first, is just how blatant the sexual imagery is and yet how totally unacknowledged as such. And so we reason that Grey, writing popular fiction in 1912, cannot present sexuality "directly," that is, through sexual intercourse between the characters, and cannot even represent characters who are conscious of having sexual desires, and so he projects desire onto the landscape instead. It may be that Grey can't even let *himself* know that sex is what he is portraying here. And that degree of repression, we infer, probably accounts for the erotic passion one finds everywhere in the novel. Not only is the landscape engorged, but the characters' looks, dress, bodily movements, and conversation are continually giving off sexual signals and pulsating with sexual energy.

Although this account of the passage—based loosely on Freudian psychology—makes sense on its own terms, I think it crucially misses what Grey has to offer. Our habitual mode of psychological explanation takes it for granted that human beings are bounded entities surrounded by a nonhuman world of objects, and that these entities operate according to a hydraulic system in which energy blocked in one place breaks forth in another. The very vocabulary of *repression, sublimation, projection,* and *displacement* domesticates the content of passages like these by maintaining the boundaries between self and world that Grey is transgressing and, in effect, explaining away the very phenomena he is always realizing. The power of the "notched bulge" passage lies in the suggestion that sexuality pervades the universe, is not subjective, and belongs as much to the rim rock and the thicket as to Venters and the girl. Nor is it sexuality alone that we are dealing with here. Sexual passion in Grey passes continually in and out of grief, rage, frustration, vengeance, longing, and other, unnameable feelings, which sweep through the life-world of the novel in a continual kaleidoscope of desire. In Grey's prose you have a sense of energy on the loose, not tethered anywhere, not belonging to any one person or thing, not subject to rules, not exactly familiar and not quite alien either, and this produces feelings of danger and exhilaration so strong that at times reading his prose is like riding a horse that is barely under control. Which is exactly what is happening in some of the most breathtaking passages of his fiction.

To speak of the landscape as a dynamic agent in Grey's fiction, having a life of its own that is yet not distinct from the life of the human agents, is not to speak metaphorically. At the end of the novel, the land's upflinging, heaving tendencies explode to form the climax of the plot, as the fall of Balancing Rock literally seals the protagonists' fate:

It stirred, it groaned, it grated, it moved; and with a slow grinding, as of wrathful relief, began to lean. It had waited ages to fall, and now was slow in starting. Then, as if suddenly instinct with life, it leaped hurtlingly down to alight on the steep incline, to bound more swiftly into the air, to gather momentum, to plunge into the lofty leaning crag below. The crag thundered into atoms. A wave of air—a splitting shock! Dust shrouded the sunset red of shaking rims; dust shrouded Tull as he fell on his knees with uplifted arms. Shafts and monuments and sections of wall fell majestically.

From the depths there arose a long-drawn rumbling roar. The outlet to Deception Pass closed forever. (280)

In this orgasmic act of self-destruction, a long-awaited moment of "wrathful relief" that ends in dust and shrouds, the landscape expresses feelings that are too colossal, too outrageous, and too inexplicable for human characters to claim. Wreaking a horrible vengeance on the villain, forcing the hero and heroine to come together, the fall of Balancing Rock commits murder and sexual intercourse at the same time. I do not think this is an exaggeration. Grey's fiction derives its depth and power from the embodiment of passions whose forbidden character and immense proportions cannot be expressed by human beings but demand a superhuman, almost ultramundane form.

The landscape in *Riders of the Purple Sage* is described by Grey and experienced by his characters with such intensity that it does not seem any longer to be purely physical. Continuous with the human figures who people it and invested with psychic energy, nature moves and heaves, plummets and rises up, explodes, contracts, swerves back on itself, in corporeal enactment of passions that have no beginning and no end. In reading this fiction we are always in a state of transformation passing from matter into energy and back into matter again, from tenderness into rage and thence to grief and longing, from interior to exterior to interior to exterior and back again. Instead of there being a world of internal states and feelings on the one hand, and of external objects, places, events on the other, there is only a single medium that is labile, metamorphic.

Metamorphosis is what the novel strives for and enacts at every level. You can see it not only in the relation between character and landscape, but also in the constant boundary crossing that takes place within and between characters, as in the novel's first scene. Everything is anticipated here. At the outset, Jane Withersteen, the heroine, is about to watch the Mormon elders whip her best rider, whom they are persecuting because they want to weaken Jane's hold on her ranch. Suddenly a rider appears out of the sage; it is Lassiter, the famous gunman, arrived just in time to save the heroine. The passage immediately preceding Lassiter's arrival contains one of those moments of boundary crossing so frequent in Grey which signal that something important is happening. This time several boundaries are crossed at once. Just before Lassiter appears, Jane is about to give up:

> Her head was bowing to the inevitable. She was grasping the truth, when suddenly there came, in inward constriction, a hardening of gentle forces within her breast. Like a steel bar it was, stiffening all that had been soft and weak in her. She felt a birth in her of something new and unintelligible. Once more her strained gaze sought the sage-slopes. (7–8)

The next thing we know, Lassiter appears out of the sage: he *is* the "something new and unintelligible" the heroine feels forming inside her. Embryo and phallus, stiffening, hardening, "like a steel bar," he represents the birth of something masculine in Jane: her resistance to authority, the will to commit violence. Jane's metamorphosis into a man-woman involves the breaching of several boundaries: the line that divides bodies from each other (Lassiter's from Jane's), that delineates gender categories (male and female), and that separates discrete moments in time (in this initial transformation, Jane has already brought to birth everything the narrative will eventually labor to produce). But the transformation also represents a historic moment.

Photograph of Zane Grey writing.
Courtesy of Loren Grey.

The hero and heroine of *Riders of the Purple Sage* act out a drama that is not merely personal or sexual. They dramatize something that might almost be described as the zeitgeist in combat with itself. Jane Withersteen, modeled on the heroine of the nineteenth-century sentimental novel, encapsulates fifty years of Victorian piety and domesticity. She believes in spiritual salvation and in Christian love and forgiveness, in self-effacement, obedience to authority, and the sanctity of the family. She dresses in white, loves children, serves the poor, and fights against her own anger. *Riders of the Purple Sage* is told largely from her point of view and is intently focused on the inner struggles of its characters. It draws morally and structurally on the strengths of sentimental fiction.

Lassiter, the Western hero, stands for everything Jane stands against—secularism, individual rights, retributive justice, and the ultimate reality of matter and physical force. The "birth" that takes place within the heroine, partly against her will, is the birth of Lassiter's child—the twentieth century. His coming represents the triumph of everything that "masculinity" has traditionally been made to represent in our time, especially the belief that physical force rather than faith or love is the might that will save us, and its corollary, the legitimization of physical violence. Lassiter is our teacher in this book. He has come to the rescue, Jane's and ours. He teaches Jane, and us through her, that we must be a man and take up the gun. The "something new and unintelligible" Jane feels forming inside her is the twentieth century.

But the novel struggles against this birth at every step. What has made it live and given it so much power in our culture is the way it moves back and forth between the two life-worlds, represented by Jane and Lassiter, never resting in either but giving each, over and over, its emotional day in court. The world of Jane Withersteen and the world of Lassiter are in continual conflict. Each represents a whole complex of values and beliefs which Grey alternately embraces and rejects. In a series of scenes in which Jane struggles to overcome her anger, we feel Grey's admiration for the selflessness and devotion to others she stands for. She is swept by surges of anger that have the power of natural forces to devastate and consume: "She went stone-blind in the fury of a passion that had never before showed its power. Lying upon her bed, sightless, voiceless, she was a writhing, living flame. And she tossed there while her fury burned . . . " (61). What makes Jane great in Grey's eyes is that she can conquer the hate in herself and rise above it. "She had knelt by her bedside and prayed; she prayed as she had never prayed in all her life . . . to be immune from that dark, hot hate . . . to do her duty by her church and people . . . to hold reverence of God and womanhood inviolate" (61). Again and again, Jane's anger leaps out: "Her passion, like fire at white heat, consumed itself in little time" (252). In a supreme moment, when Jane learns that Venters has been living with Bess in Surprise Valley, she not only rises above her anger but replaces it with love and generosity, giving Venters her last and most prized possessions—her horses, Black Star and Night.

> Then in the white, rapt face, in the unfathomable eyes, Venters saw Jane Withersteen in a supreme moment. This moment was one wherein she reached up to the height for which her noble soul had ever yearned. . . . Jane Withersteen was the incarnation of selflessness. (260)

But the very qualities Grey admires so much in Jane are also the source of his ambivalence toward her. The glory of self-conquest, which emerges in Jane's dealing with Venters, hides the dangers of her self-deception, which come out in her treatment of Lassiter. On the battleground of sex, self-conquest becomes repression, veiling strategies of domination and control. Jane uses her sexuality to bind Lassiter to her and gain control of the violent power he represents, while denying to herself her own desire to be and act as he does. In Jane Withersteen, though she does not know it, her desire to control Lassiter and *his* desire to kill her enemies are intertwined:

> "I can head them all with this hoss, an' then—"
>
> "Then, Lassiter?"

"They'll never stampede no more cattle."

"Oh! No! . . . Lassiter, I won't let you go!"

But a flush of fire flamed in her cheeks, and her trembling hands shook Black Star's bridle, and her eyes fell before Lassiter's. (70)

Jane is excited by Lassiter as killer. Her touching of Black Star's bridle alludes to the way horses mediate between the savior and killer sides of herself. In accepting her love for Lassiter (who, she jokingly says, is "half-horse") she has to accept her love of the violence he commits. Her final words to him—"Lassiter, I love you! *Roll the stone!* "—represent the union of love and murder in her heart (280).

These struggles and blindnesses are, of course, Grey's own. In his drive to retrieve the "savage" part of himself, linking the caveman and God, Grey makes his heroine embrace a murderer. But the murderer is also compact with conflicting elements. At one point in the novel, Lassiter decides to renounce his "passion for blood," takes off his guns, and offers them to Jane:

I give up my purpose. I've come to see an' feel differently. . . . I've outgrown revenge. I've come to see I can't be no judge for men. I can't kill a man just for hate. Hate ain't the same thing with me since I loved you and little Fay. (233)

Softened and domesticated by a good woman, Lassiter asks Jane to go away with him to where he can "put away [his] guns and be a man" (226–27). Lassiter's announcement that manhood lies in giving up his guns contradicts a moment earlier in the novel when Venters had declared, taking his guns back from Jane, that he could only be a man *with* them.

These antithetical moments do not so much confuse the issue of where ultimate manhood lies as they dramatize the monumental upheaval, both cultural and psychological, that the novel is in the business of portraying. In the nineteenth century, Christian renunciation and doing one's duty to society constituted heroic behavior; in the coming era, virtue assumes a more extroverted, dynamic, and material form. The larger-than-life characters the novel pits against one another are acting out alternatives within the cultural unconscious.

The use of a term like *unconscious* reminds us that the turn of the century brought with it seismic shifts in almost every cultural sphere. Christianity gives way to a variety of secular faiths (Freudian psychology, scientific rationalism, liberal humanism); technology alters human beings' relation to the physical world and to daily work; the conception of human sexuality and of gender roles undergoes drastic revision, and with these changes come new forms of social behavior, different ways of conceiving the self and imagining the aims of human life. Something of all these changes is being registered in the tumultuous struggles within and between Grey's characters, in the ideological flip-flopping of the narrative as Grey takes up now one position, now the other, and in the metamorphic nature of the landscape the characters inhabit. Only Utah's gargantuan body is capable of expressing vicissitudes like these. Grey doesn't know that he is making the rim rock and the sage slopes enact the birth of a new age, but that is what he is doing.

The land is never represented in Westerns in this way again. Because of the moment in which he was writing, a moment *between* the nineteenth and twentieth centuries, Grey had access simultaneously to ways of feeling and thinking and to modes of expression that now seem diametrically opposed but that existed then, for him, in an immensely fertile if unstable equilibrium. Their combination produced a prose that seems to promise possibilities of transformation that were never subsequently realized. In the Western novels and movies that succeed Grey's, the landscape hardens. Appealing to the soul of the twentieth century, and reflecting the aesthetics of modernism, the empty spaces and lonely buttes of the classical Western depict a phallic landscape of death. Monument Valley is its ideal mise-en-scène. There is no change here and, correspondingly, no inward human commotion. Lassiter is there, but Jane is gone, and with her the chance for transformation. No Surprise Valley or Deception Pass, no lava flow; in place of metamorphosis and volcanic eruption, the lone and level sands stretch far away.

Photograph of Buffalo Bill.
Courtesy of the Buffalo Bill Memorial Museum and the Denver Parks
and Recreation Department, Denver, Colorado.

At the Buffalo Bill Museum ☆ June 1988

9

The video at the entrance to the Buffalo Bill Historical Center says that Buffalo Bill was the most famous American of his time, that by 1900 more than a billion words had been written about him, and that he had a progressive vision of the West. Buffalo Bill had worked as a cattle driver, a wagoneer, a Pony Express rider, a buffalo hunter for the railroad, a hunting guide, an army scout and some-time Indian fighter; he wrote dime novels about himself and an autobiography by the age of thirty-four, by which time he was already famous; and then he began another set of careers, first as an actor, performing on the urban stage in wintertime melodramatic repre-sentations of what he actually earned a living at in the summer (scouting and leading hunting expeditions), and finally becoming the impresario of his great Wild West show, a form of entertainment he invented and carried on as actor, director, and all-around idea man for thirty years. Toward the end of his life he founded the town of Cody, Wyoming, to which he gave, among other things, two hundred thousand dollars. Strangely enough, it was as a pro-gressive civic leader that Bill Cody wanted to be remembered. "I don't want to die," the video at the entrance quotes him as saying, "and have people say—oh, there goes another old showman. . . . I would like people to say—this is man who opened Wyoming to the best of civilization."

"The best of civilization." This was the phrase that rang in my head as I moved through the museum, which is one of the most disturbing places I have ever visited. It is also a wonderful place. It is four museums in one: the Whitney Gallery of Western Art, which houses artworks on Western subjects; the Buffalo Bill Museum proper, which memorializes Cody's life; the Plains Indian Museum, which exhibits artifacts of American Indian civilization; and the Winchester Arms Museum, a collection of firearms historically considered.

The whole operation is extremely well designed and well run, from the video program at the entrance that gives an overview of all four museums, to the fresh-faced young attendants wearing badges that say "Ask Me," to the museum shop stacked with books on Western Americana, to the ladies room—a haven of satiny marble, shining mirrors, and flattering light. Among other things, the museum is admirable for its effort to combat prevailing stereotypes about the "winning of the West," a phrase it self-consciously places in quotation marks. There are placards declaring that all history is a matter of interpretation, and that the American West is a source of myth. Everywhere, except perhaps in the Winchester Arms Museum, where the rhetoric is different, you feel the effort of the museum staff to reach out to the public, to be clear, to be accurate, to be fair, not to condescend—in short, to educate in the best sense of the term.

On the day I went, the museum was featuring an exhibition of Frederic Remington's works. Two facts about Remington make his work different from that of artists usually encountered in museums. The first is that Remington's paintings and statues function as a historical record. Their chief attraction has always been that they transcribe scenes and events that have vanished from the earth. The second fact, related to this, is the brutality of their subject matter. Remington's work makes you pay attention to what is happening in the painting or the piece of statuary. When you look at his work you cannot escape from the subject.

Consequently, as I moved through the exhibit, the wild contortions of the bucking broncos, the sinister expression invariably worn by the Indians, and the killing of animals and men made the placards discussing Remington's use of the "lost wax" process seem strangely disconnected. In the face of unusual violence, or implied violence, their message was: what is important here is technique. Except in the case of paintings showing the battle of San Juan Hill, where white Americans were being killed, the material accompanying Remington's works did not refer to the subject matter of the paintings and statues themselves. Nevertheless, an undertone of disquiet ran beneath the explanations; at least I thought I detected one. Someone had taken the trouble to ferret out Remington's statement of horror at the slaughter on San Juan Hill; someone had also excerpted the judgment of art critics commending Remington for the lyricism, interiority, and mystery of his later canvasses—pointing obliquely to the fascination with bloodshed that preoccupied his earlier work.

The uneasiness of the commentary, and my uneasiness with it, were nothing compared to the blatant contradictions in the paintings themselves. A pastel palette, a sunlit stop-action haze, murderous movement arrested under a lazy sky, flattened onto canvas and fixed in azure and ochre—two opposed impulses nestle here momentarily. The tension that keeps them from splitting apart is what holds the viewer's gaze.

The most excruciating example of what I mean occurs in the first painting in the exhibit. Entitled *His First Lesson*, it shows a horse standing saddled but riderless, the white of the horse's eye signaling his fear. A man using an instrument to tighten the horse's girth, at arm's length, backs away from the reaction he clearly anticipates, while the man who holds the horse's halter is doing the same. But what can they be afraid of? For the horse's right rear leg is tied a foot off the ground by a rope that is also tied around his neck. He can't move. That is the whole point.

His First Lesson. Whose? And what lesson, exactly? How to

"His First Lesson," by Frederic Remington, 1903. Oil on canvas.
Courtesy of the Amon Carter Museum, Fort Worth, Texas (accession no. 1961.231).

stand still when terrified? How not to break away when they come at you with strange instruments? How to be obedient? How to behave? It is impossible not to imagine that Remington's obsession with physical cruelty had roots somewhere in his own experience. Why else, in statue after statue, is the horse rebelling? The bucking bronco, symbol of the state of Wyoming, on every licence plate, on every sign for every bar, on every belt buckle, mug, and decal— this image Remington cast in bronze over and over again. There is a wild diabolism in the bronzes; the horse and rider seem one thing, not so much rider and ridden as a single bolt of energy gone crazy and caught somehow, complicatedly, in a piece of metal.

In the paintings, it is different—more subtle and bizarre. The cavalry on its way to a massacre, sweetly limned, softly tinted, poetically seized in mid-career, and gently laid on the two-dimensional surface. There is about these paintings of military men in the course of performing their deadly duty an almost maternal tenderness. The idealization of the cavalrymen in their dusty uniforms on their gallant horses has nothing to do with patriotism; it is pure love.

Remington's paintings and statues, as shown in this exhibition, embody everything that was objectionable about his era in American history. They are imperialist and racist; they glorify war and the torture and killing of animals; there are no women in them anywhere. Never the West as garden, never as pastoral, never as home. But in their aestheticization of violent life, Remington's pictures speak (to me, at least) of some other desire. The maternal tenderness is not an accident, nor is the beauty of the afternoons or the warmth of the desert sun. In them Remington plays the part of the preserver, as if by catching the figures in color and line he could save their lives and absorb some of that life into himself.

In one painting that particularly repulsed and drew me, a moose is outlined against the evening sky at the brink of a lake. He looks expectantly into the distance. Behind him and to one side, hidden from his view and only just revealed to ours, for it is dark there, is a hunter poised in the back of a canoe, rifle perfectly aimed. We look closer; the title of the picture is *Coming to the Call*. Ah, now we see. This is a sadistic scene. The hunter has lured the moose to his death. But wait a moment. Isn't the sadism really directed at us? First we see the glory of the animal; Remington has made it as noble as he knows how. Then we see what is going to happen. The hunter is one up on the moose, but Remington is one up on us. He makes us feel the pain of the anticipated killing, and makes us want to hold it off, to preserve the moose, just as he has done. Which way does the painting cut? Does it go against the hunter—who represents us, after all— or does it go against the moose who came to the call? Who came, to what call? Did Remington come to the West in response to it—to whatever the moose represents or to whatever the desire to kill the moose represents? But he hasn't killed it; he has only preserved an image of a white man about to kill it. And what call do we answer when we look at this painting? Who is calling whom? What is being preserved here?

That last question is the one that for me hung over the whole museum.

The Whitney Gallery is an art museum proper. Its allegiance is to art as academic tradition has defined it. In this tradition, we come to understand a painting by having in our possession various bits of information. Something about the technical process used to produce it (pastels, watercolors, woodblock prints, etc.); something about the elements of composition (line and color and movement); something about the artist's life (where born, how educated, by whom influenced, which school belonged to or revolted against); something about the artist's relation to this particular subject, such as how many times the artist painted it or whether it contains a favorite model. Occasionally there will be some philosophizing about the themes or ideas the paintings are said to represent.

The problem is, when you're faced with a painter like Remington, these bits of information, while nice to have, don't explain what is there in front of you. They don't begin to give you an account of why a person should have depicted such things. The experience of a lack of fit between the explanatory material and what is there on the wall is one I've had before in museums, when, standing in front of a painting or a piece of statuary, I've felt a huge gap between the information on the little placard and what it is I'm seeing. I realize that works of art, so-called, all have a subject matter, are all engaged with life, with some piece of life no less significant, no less compelling than Remington's subjects are, if we could only see its force. The idea that art is somehow separate from history, that it somehow occupies a space that is not the same as the space of life, seems out of whack here.

I wandered through the gallery thinking these things because right next to it, indeed all around it, in the Buffalo Bill Museum proper and in the Plains Indian Museum, are artifacts that stand not for someone's expertise or skill in manipulating the elements of an artistic medium, but for life itself; they are the residue of life.

The Buffalo Bill Museum is a wonderful array of textures, colors, shapes, sizes, forms. The fuzzy brown bulk of a buffalo's hump, the sparkling diamonds in a stickpin, the brilliant colors of the posters—the mixture makes you want to walk in and be surrounded by it, as if you were going into a child's adventure story. For a moment you can pretend you're a cowboy too; it's a museum where fantasy can take over. For a while.

As I moved through the exhibition, with the phrase "the best of civilization" ringing in my head, I came upon certain objects displayed in a section that recreates rooms from Cody's house. Ostrich feather fans, peacock feather fans, antler furniture—a chair and a table made entirely of antlers—a bearskin rug. And then I saw the heads on the wall: Alaska Yukon Moose, Wapiti American Elk, Muskox (the "Whitney," the "DeRham"), Mountain Caribou (the "Hyland"), Quebec Labrador Caribou (the "Elbow"), Rocky Mountain Goat (the "Haase," the "Kilto"), Woodland Caribou (world's record, "DeRham"), the "Rogers" freak Wapiti, the "Whitney" bison, the "Lord Rundlesham" bison. The names that appear after the animals are the names of the men who killed them. Each of the animals is scored according to measurements devised by the Boone and Crockett Club, a big-game hunters' organization. The Lord Rundlesham bison, for example, scores 124⅝, making it number 25 in the world for bison trophies. The "Reed" Alaska Yukon Moose scores 247. The "Witherbee" Canada moose holds the world's record.

Next to the wall of trophies is a small enclosure where jewelry is displayed. A buffalo head stickpin and two buffalo head rings, the heads made entirely of diamonds, with ruby eyes, the gifts of the Russian crown prince. A gold and diamond stickpin from Edward VII; a gold, diamond, and garnet locket from Queen Victoria. The two kinds of trophies—animals and jewels—form an incongruous set; the relationship between them compelling but obscure.

If the rest of the items in the museum—the dime novels with their outrageous covers, the marvelous posters, the furniture, his wife's dress, his daughter's oil painting—have faded from my mind it is because I cannot forget the heads of the animals as they stared down, each with an individual expression on its face. When I think about it I realize that I don't know why these animal heads are there. Buffalo Bill didn't kill them; perhaps they were gifts from the famous people he took on hunts. A different kind of jewelry.

After the heads, I began to notice something about the whole exhibition. In one display, doghide chaps, calfskin chaps, angora goathide chaps, and horsehide chaps. Next to these a rawhide lariat and a horsehair quirt. Behind me, boots and saddles, all of leather. Everywhere I looked there was tooth or bone, skin or fur, hide or hair, or the animal itself entire—two full-size buffalo (a main feature of the exhibition) and a magnificent stone sheep (a mountain sheep with beautiful curving horns). This one was another world's record. The best of civilization.

In the literature about Buffalo Bill you read that he was a conservationist, that if it were not for the buffalo in his Wild West shows the species would probably have become extinct. (In the seventeenth century 40 million buffalo roamed North America; by 1900 all the wild buffalo had been killed except for one herd in northern Alberta.) That the man who gained fame first as a buffalo hunter should have been an advocate for conservation of the buffalo is not an anomaly but typical of the period. The men who did the most to preserve America's natural wilderness and its wildlife were big-game hunters. The Boone and Crockett Club, founded by Theodore Roosevelt, George Bird Grinnell, and Owen Wister, turns out to have been one of the earliest organizations to devote itself to environmental protection in the United States. *The Reader's Encyclopedia of the American West* says that the club "supported the national park and forest reserve movement, helped create a system of national wildlife refuges, and lobbied for the protection of threatened species, such as the buffalo and antelope." At the same time, the prerequisites for membership in the club were "the highest caliber of sportsmanship and the achievement of killing 'in fair chase' trophy specimens [which had to be adult males] from several species of North American big game."

The combination big-game hunter and conservationist suggests that these men had no interest in preserving the animals for the animals' sake but simply wanted to ensure the chance to exercise their sporting pleasure. But I think this view is too simple; something further is involved here. The men who hunted game animals had a kind of love for them and a kind of love for nature that led them to want to preserve the animals they also desired to kill. That is, the desire to kill the animals was in some way related to a desire to see them live. It is not an accident, in this connection, that Roosevelt, Wister, and Remington all went west originally for their health. Their devotion to the West, their connection to it, their love for it are rooted in their need to reanimate their own lives. The preservation of nature, in other words, becomes for them symbolic of their own survival.

In a sense, then, there is a relationship between the Remington exhibition in the Whitney Gallery and the animal memorabilia in the Buffalo Bill Museum. The moose in *Coming to the Call* and the mooseheads on the wall are not so different as they might appear. The heads on the wall serve an aesthetic purpose; they are decorative objects, pleasing to the eye, which call forth certain associations. In this sense they are like visual works of art. The painting, on the other hand, has something of the trophy about it. The moose as Remington painted it is about to become a trophy, yet in another sense it already is one. Remington has simply captured the moose in another form. In both cases the subject matter, the life of a wild animal, symbolizes the life of the observer. It is the preservation of that life that both the painting and the taxidermy serve.

What are museums keeping safe for us, after all? What is it that we wish so much to preserve? The things we put in safekeeping, in our safe-deposit boxes under lock and key, are always in some way intended finally as safeguards of our own existence. The money and jewelry and stock certificates are meant for a time when we can no longer earn a living by the sweat of our brows. Similarly, the objects in museums preserve for us a source of life from which we need to nourish ourselves when the resources that would normally supply us have run dry.

The Buffalo Bill Historical Center, full as it is of dead bones, lets us see more clearly than we normally can what it is that museums are for. It is a kind of charnel house that houses images of living things that have passed away but whose life force still lingers around their remains and so passes itself on to us. We go and look at the objects in the glass cases and at the paintings on the wall, as if by standing there we could absorb into ourselves some of the energy that flowed once through the bodies of the live things represented. A museum, rather than being, as we normally think of it, the most civilized of places, a place most distant from our savage selves, actually caters to the urge to absorb the life of another into one's own life.

If we see the Buffalo Bill Museum in this way, it is no longer possible to separate ourselves from the hunters responsible for the trophies with their wondering eyes or from the curators who put them there. We are not, in essence, different from Roosevelt or Remington or Buffalo Bill, who killed animals when they were abundant in the Wild West of the 1880s. If in doing so those men were practicing the ancient art of absorbing the life of an animal into their own through the act of killing it, realizing themselves through the destruction of another life, then we are not so different from them, as visitors to the museum, we stand beside the bones and skins and nails of beings that were once alive, or stare fixedly at their painted images. Indeed our visit is only a safer form of the same enterprise as theirs.

So I did not get out of the Buffalo Bill Museum unscathed, unimplicated in the acts of rapine and carnage that these remains represent. And I did not get out without having had a good time, either, because however many dire thoughts I may have had, the exhibits were interesting and fun to see. I was even able to touch a piece of buffalo hide displayed especially for that purpose (it was coarse and springy). Everyone else had touched it too. The hair was worn down, where people's hands had been, to a fraction of its original length.

After this, the Plains Indian Museum was a terrible letdown. I went from one exhibit to another expecting to become absorbed, but nothing worked. What was the matter? I was interested in Indians, had read about them, taught some Indian literature, felt drawn by accounts of native religions. I had been prepared to enter this museum as if I were going into another children's story, only this time I would be an Indian instead of a cowboy or a cowgirl. But the objects on display, most of them behind glass, seemed paltry and insignificant. They lacked visual presence. The bits of leather and sticks of wood triggered no fantasies in me.

At the same time, I noticed with some discomfort that almost everything in those glass cases was made of feathers and claws and hide, just like the men's chaps and ladies' fans in the Buffalo Bill Museum, only there was no luxury here. Plains Indian culture, it seemed, was made entirely from animals. Their mode of life had been even more completely dedicated to carnage than Buffalo Bill's, dependent as it was on animals for food, clothing, shelter, equipment, everything. In the Buffalo Bill Museum I was able to say to myself, well, if these men had been more sensitive, if they had had a right relation to their environment and to life itself, the atrocities that produced these trophies would never have occurred. They never would have exterminated the Indians and killed off the buffalo. But the spectacle before me made it impossible to say that. I had expected that the Plains Indian Museum would show me how life in nature ought to be lived: not the mindless destruction of nineteenth-century America but an ideal form of communion with animals and the land. What the museum seemed to say instead was that cannibalism was universal. Both colonizer and colonized had had their hands imbrued with blood. The Indians had lived off animals and had made war against one another. Violence was simply a necessary and inevitable part of life. And a person who, like me, was horrified at the extent of the destruction was just the kind of romantic idealist my husband sometimes accused me of being. There was no such thing as the life lived in harmony with nature. It was all bloodshed and killing, an unending cycle, over and over again, and no one could escape.

But perhaps there was a way to understand the violence that made it less terrible. Perhaps if violence was necessary, a part of nature, intended by the universe, then it could be seen as sacramental. Perhaps it was true, what Calvin Martin had said in *Keepers of the Game:* that the Indians had a sacred contract with the animals they killed, that they respected them as equals and treated their remains with honor and punctilio. If so, the remains of animals in the Plains Indian Museum weren't the same as those left by Buffalo Bill and his friends. They certainly didn't look the same. Perhaps. All I knew for certain was that these artifacts, lifeless and shrunken, spoke to me of nothing I could understand. No more did the life-size models of Indians, with strange featureless faces, draped in costumes that didn't look like clothing. The figures, posed awkwardly in front of tepees too white to seem real, carried no sense of a life actually lived, any more than the objects in the glass cases had.

The more I read the placards on the wall, the more disaffected I became. Plains Indian life apparently had been not only bloody but exceedingly tedious. All those porcupine quills painstakingly softened, flattened, dyed, then appliqued through even more laborious methods of stitching or weaving. Four methods of attaching porcupine quills, six design groups, population statistics, patterns of migration. There wasn't any glamour here at all. No glamour in the lives the placards told about, no glamour in the objects themselves, no glamour in the experience of looking at them. Just a lot of shriveled things accompanied by some even drier information.

Could it be, then, that the problem with the exhibitions was that Plains Indian culture, if representable at all, was simply not readable by someone like me? Their stick figures and abstract designs could convey very little to an untrained Euro-American eye. One display in particular illustrated this. It was a piece of cloth, behind glass, depicting a buffalo skin with some marks on it. The placard read: "Winter Count, Sioux ca. 1910, after Lone Dog's, Fort Peck, Montana, 1877." The hide with its markings had been a calendar, each year represented by one image, which showed the most significant event in the life of the tribe. A thick pamphlet to one side of the glass case explained each image year by year: 1800–1801, the attack of the Uncapoo on a Crow Indian Fort; 1802–1803, a total eclipse of the sun. The images, once you knew what they represented, made sense, and seemed poetic interpretations of the experiences they stood for. But without explanation they were incomprehensible.

The Plains Indian Museum stopped me in my tracks. It was written in a language I had never learned. I didn't have the key. Maybe someone did, but I wasn't too sure. For it may not have been just cultural difference that made the text unreadable. I began to suspect that the text itself was corrupt, that the architects of this museum were going through motions whose purpose was, even to themselves, obscure. Knowing what event a figure stands for in the calendar doesn't mean you understand an Indian year. The deeper purpose of the museum began to puzzle me. Wasn't there an air of bad faith about preserving the vestiges of a culture one had effectively extinguished? Did the museum exist to assuage our guilt and not for any real educational reason? I do not have an answer to these questions. All I know is that I felt I was in the presence of something pious and a little insincere. It had the aura of a failed attempt at virtue, as though the curators were trying to present as interesting objects whose purpose and meaning even they could not fully imagine.

In a last-ditch attempt to salvage something, I went up to one of the guards and asked where the movie was showing which the video had advertised, the movie about Plains Indian life. "Oh, the slide show, you mean," he said. "It's been discontinued." When I asked why, he said he didn't know. It occurred to me then that that was the message the museum was sending, if I could read it, that that was the bottom line. Discontinued, no reason given.

The movie in the Winchester Arms Museum, *Lock, Stock, and Barrel*, was going strong. The film began with the introduction of cannon into European warfare in the Middle Ages, and was working its way slowly toward the nineteenth century when I left. I was in a hurry. Soon my husband would be waiting for me in the lobby.

I went from room to room, trying to get a quick sense impression of the objects on display. They were all the same: guns. Some large drawings and photographs on the walls tried to give a sense of the context in which the arms had been used, but the effect was nil. It was case after case of rifles and pistols, repeating themselves over and over, and even when some slight variation caught my eye the differences meant nothing to me.

But the statistics did. In a large case of commemorative rifles, I saw the Antlered Game Commemorative Carbine. Date of manufacture: 1978. Number produced: 19,999. I wondered how many antlered animals each carbine had killed. I saw the Canadian Centennial (1962): 90,000; the Legendary Lawman (1978): 19,999; the John Wayne (1980–81): 51,600. Like the titles of the various sections of the museum, these names had a message. The message was: guns are patriotic. Associated with national celebrations, law enforcement, and cultural heroes. The idea that firearms were inseparable from the march of American history came through even more strongly in the titles given to the various exhibits: Firearms in Colonial America; Born in America: The Kentucky Rifle; The Era of Expansion and Invention; The Civil War: Firearms of the Conflict; The Golden Age of Hunting; Winning the West. The guns embodied phases of the history they had helped to make. There were no quotation marks here to indicate that expansion and conquest might not have been all they were cracked up to be. The fact that firearms had had a history seemed to consecrate them; the fact that they had existed at the time when certain famous events had occurred seemed to make them not only worth preserving but worth studying and revering. In addition to the exhibition rooms, the museum housed three "study galleries": one for hand arms, one for shoulder arms, one for U.S. military firearms.

As I think back on the rows and rows of guns, I wonder if I should have looked at them more closely, tried harder to appreciate the workmanship that went into them, the ingenuity, the attention.

Awe and admiration are the attitudes the museum invites. You hear the ghostly march of military music in the background; you imagine flags waving and sense the implicit reference to feats of courage in battle and glorious death. The place had the air of an expensive and well-kept reliquary, or of the room off the transept of a cathedral where the vestments are stored. These guns were not there merely to be seen or even studied; they were there to be venerated.

But I did not try to appreciate the guns. They were too technical, too foreign. I didn't have their language, and, besides, I didn't want to learn. I rejoined my husband in the lobby. The Plains Indian Museum had been incomprehensible, but in the Winchester Arms Museum I could hardly see the objects at all, for I did not see the point. Or, rather, I did see it and rejected it. Here in the basement the instruments that had turned live animals into hides and horns, had massacred the Indians and the buffalo, were being lovingly displayed. And we were still making them: 51,600 John Waynes in 1980–81. Arms were going strong.

As I bought my books and postcards in the gift shop, I noticed a sign that read "Rodeo Tickets Sold Here," and something clicked into place. So that was it. *Everything* was still going strong. The whole museum was just another rodeo, only with the riders and their props stuffed, painted, sculpted, immobilized and put under glass. Like the rodeo, the entire museum witnessed a desire to bring back the United States of the 1880s and 1890s. The American people did not want to let go of the winning of the West. They wanted to win it all over again, in imagination. It was the ecstasy of the kill, as much as the life of the hunted, that we fed off here. The Buffalo Bill Historical Center did not repudiate the carnage that had taken place in the nineteenth century. It celebrated it. With its gleaming rest rooms, cute snack bar, opulent museum shop, wooden Indians, thousand rifles, and scores of animal trophies, it helped us all reenact the dream of excitement, adventure, and conquest that was what the Wild West meant to most people in this country.

This is where my visit ended, but it had a sequel. When I left the Buffalo Bill Historical Center, I was full of moral outrage, an indignation so intense it made me almost sick, though it was pleasurable too, as such emotions usually are. But the outrage was undermined by the knowledge that I knew nothing about Buffalo Bill, nothing of his life, nothing of the circumstances that led him to be involved in such violent events. And I began to wonder if my reaction wasn't in some way an image, however small, of the violence I had been objecting to. So when I got home I began to read about Buffalo Bill, and a whole new world opened up. I came to love Buffalo Bill.

"I have seen him the very personification of grace and beauty . . . dashing over the free wild prairie and riding his horse as though he and the noble animal were bounding with one life and one motion." That is the sort of thing people wrote about Buffalo Bill. They said "he was the handsomest man I ever saw." They said "there was never another man lived as popular as he was." They said "there wasn't a man woman or child that he knew or ever met that he didn't speak to." They said "he was handsome as a god, a good rider and a crack shot." They said "he gave lots of money away. Nobody ever went hungry around him." They said "he was way above the average, physically and every other way."

These are quotes from people who knew Cody, collected by one of his two most responsible biographers, Nellie Snyder Yost. She puts them in the last chapter, and by the time you get there they all ring true. Buffalo Bill was incredibly handsome. He was extremely brave and did things no other scout would do. He would carry messages over rugged territory swarming with hostile Indians, riding all night in bad weather and get through, and then take off again the next day to ride sixty miles through a blizzard. He was not a proud man. He didn't boast of his exploits. But he did do incredible things, not just once in a while but on a fairly regular basis. He had a great deal of courage; he believed in himself, in his abilities, in his strength and endurance and knowledge. He was very skilled at what he did—hunting and scouting—but he wasn't afraid to try other things. He wrote some dime novels, he wrote his autobiography by age thirty-four, without very much schooling; he wasn't afraid to try acting, even though the stage terrified him and he knew so little about it that, according to his wife, he didn't even know you had to memorize lines.

Maybe it was because he grew up on the frontier, maybe it was just the kind of person he was, but he was constantly finding himself in situations that required resourcefulness and courage, quick decisions and decisive action and rising to the occasion. He wasn't afraid to improvise.

He liked people, drank a lot, gave big parties, gave lots of presents, and is reputed to have been a womanizer (Cody, 16). When people came to see him in his office tent on the show grounds, to shake his hand or have their pictures taken with him, he never turned anyone away. "He kept a uniformed doorman at the tent opening to announce visitors," writes a biographer. "No matter who was outside, from a mayor to a shabby woman with a baby, the Colonel would smooth his mustache, stand tall and straight, and tell the doorman to 'show 'em in.' He greeted everyone the same" (Yost, 436).

As a showman, he was a genius. People don't say much about *why* he was so successful; mostly they describe the wonderful goings-on. But I get the feeling that Cody was one of those people who was connected to his time in an uncanny way. He knew what people wanted, he knew how to entertain them, because he *liked* them, was open to them, felt his kinship with them, or was so much in touch with himself at some level that he was thereby in touch with almost everybody else.

He liked to dress up and had a great sense of costume (of humor, too, they say). Once he came to a fancy dress ball, his first, in New York, wearing white tie and tails and a large Stetson. He knew what people wanted. He let his hair grow long and wore a mustache and beard, because, he said, he wouldn't be believable as a scout otherwise. Hence his Indian name, Pahaska, meaning "long hair," which people loved to use. Another kind of costume. He invented the ten-gallon hat, which the Stetson company made to his specifications. Afterward, they made a fortune from it. In the scores of pictures reproduced in the many books about him, he most often wears scout's clothes—usually generously fringed buckskin, sometimes a modified cavalryman's outfit—though often he's impeccably turned out in a natty-looking three-piece business suit (sometimes with overcoat, sometimes not). The photographs show him in a tuxedo, in something called a "Mexican suit" which looks like a cowboy outfit, and once he appears in Indian dress. In almost every case he is wearing some kind of hat, usually the Stetson, at exactly the right angle. He poses deliberately, and with dignity, for the picture. Cody didn't take himself so seriously that he had to pretend to be less than he was.

What made Buffalo Bill so irresistible? Why is he still so appealing, even now, when we've lost, supposedly, all the illusions that once supported his popularity? There's a poster for one of his shows when he was traveling in France that gives a clue to what it is that makes him so profoundly attractive a figure. The poster consists of a huge buffalo galloping across the plains, and against the buffalo's hump, in the center of his hump, is a cutout circle that shows the head of Buffalo Bill, white-mustachioed and bearded now, in his famous hat, and beneath, in large red letters, are the words "Je viens."

Je viens ("I am coming") are the words of a savior. The an-

"Je Viens," c. 1900. Color lithograph.
Courtesy of the Buffalo Bill Historical Center, Cody, Wyoming.

nouncement is an annunciation. Buffalo Bill is a religious figure of a kind who makes sense within a specifically Christian tradition. That is, he comes in the guise of a redeemer, of someone who will save us, who will through his own actions do something for us that we ourselves cannot do. He will lift us above our lives, out of the daily grind, into something larger than we are.

His appeal on the surface is to childish desires, the desire for glamour, fame, bigness, adventure, romance. But these desires are also the sign of something more profound, and it is to something more profound in us that he also appeals. Buffalo Bill comes to the child in us, understood not as that part of ourselves that we have outgrown but as the part that got left behind, of necessity, a long time ago, having been starved, bound, punished, disciplined out of existence. He promises that that part of the self can live again. He has the power to promise these things because he represents the West, that geographical space of the globe that was still the realm of exploration and discovery, that was still open, that had not yet quite been tamed, when he began to play himself on the stage. He not only represented it, he *was* it. He brought the West itself with him when he came. The very Indians, the very buffalo, the very cowboys, the very cattle, the very stagecoach itself which had been memorialized in story. He performed in front of the audience the feats that had made him famous. He shot glass balls and clay pigeons out of the air with amazing rapidity. He rode his watersmooth silver stallion at full gallop. "Jesus he was a handsome man," wrote e. e. cummings in "Buffalo Bill's Defunct."

"I am coming." This appearance of Buffalo Bill, in the flesh, was akin to the apparition of a saint or of the Virgin Mary to believers. He was the incarnation of an ideal. He came to show people that what they had only imagined was really true. The West really did exist. There really were heroes who rode white horses and performed amazing feats. E. e. cummings was right to invoke the name of Jesus in his poem. Buffalo Bill was a secular messiah.

He was a messiah because people believed in him. When he died, he is reputed to have said, "Let my show go on." But he had no show at the time, so he probably didn't say that. Still, the words are prophetic because the desire for what Buffalo Bill had done had not only not died but would call forth the countless reenactments of the Wild West, from the rodeo—a direct descendant of his show—to the thousands of Western novels, movies, and television programs that comprise the Western genre in the twentieth century, a genre that came into existence as a separate category right about the time that Cody died. Don Russell maintains that the way the West exists in our minds today is largely the result of the way Cody presented it in his show. That was where people got their ideas of what the characters looked like. Though many Indian tribes wore no feathers and fought on foot, you will never see a featherless, horseless Indian warrior in the movies, because Bill employed only Sioux and other Plains tribes which had horses and traditionally wore feathered headdresses. "Similarly," he adds, "cowboys wear ten-gallon Stetsons, not because such a hat was worn in early range days, but because it was part of the costume adopted by Buffalo Bill for his show" (Russell, 470).

But the deeper legacy is elsewhere. Buffalo Bill was a person who inspired other people. What they saw in him was an aspect of themselves. It really doesn't matter whether Cody was as great as people thought him or not, because what they were responding to when he rode into the arena, erect and resplendent on his charger, was something intangible, not the man himself, but a possible way of being. William F. Cody and the Wild West triggered the emotions that had fueled the imaginative lives of people who flocked to see him, especially men and boys, who made up the larger portion of the audience. He and his cowboys played to an inward territory; a Wild West of the psyche that hungered for exercise sprang into activity when the show appeared. *Je viens* was a promise to redeem that territory, momentarily at least, from exile and oblivion. The lost parts of the self symbolized by buffalo and horses and wild men would live again for an hour while the show went on.

People adored it. Queen Victoria, who broke her custom by going to see it at all (she never went to the theater, and on the rare occasions when she wanted to see a play she had it brought to her), is supposed to have been lifted out of a twenty-five-year depression caused by the death of her husband after she saw Buffalo Bill. She liked the show so much that she saw it again, arranging for a command performance to be given at Windsor Castle the day before her Diamond Jubilee. This was the occasion when four kings rode in the Deadwood stagecoach with the Prince of Wales on top next to Buffalo Bill, who drove. No one was proof against the appeal. Ralph Blumenfeld, the London correspondent for the New York *Herald*, wrote in his diary while the show was in London that he'd had two boyhood heroes, Robin Hood and Buffalo Bill, and had delighted in Cody's stories of the Pony Express and Yellow Hand:

> Everything was done to make Cody conceited and unbearable, but he remained the simple, unassuming child of the plains who thought lords and ladies belonged in the picture books and that the story of Little Red Riding Hood was true. I rode in the Deadwood coach. It was a great evening in which I realized a good many of my boyhood dreams, for there was Buffalo Bill on his white rocking horse charger, and Annie Oakley behind him. (Weybright, 172)

Victor Weybright and Henry Blackman Sell, from whose book on the Wild West some of the foregoing information has come, dedicated their book to Buffalo Bill. It was published in 1955. Nellie Snyder Yost, whose 1979 biography is one of the two scholarly accounts of Cody's life, dedicates her book "to all those good people, living or dead, who knew and liked Buffalo Bill." Don Russell's *The Lives and Legends of Buffalo Bill* (1960), the most fact-filled scholarly biography, does not have a dedication, but in the final chapter, where he steps back to assess Cody and his influence, Russell ends by exclaiming, "What more could possibly be asked of a hero? If he was not one, who was?" (Russell, 480).

Let me now pose a few questions of my own. Must we throw out all the wonderful qualities that Cody had, the spirit of hope and emulation that he aroused in millions of people, because of the terrible judgment history has passed on the epoch of which he was part? The kinds of things he stands for—courage, daring, strength, endurance, generosity, openness to other people, love of drama, love of life, the possibility of living a life that does not deny the body and the desires of the body—are these to be declared dangerous and delusional although he manifested some of them while fighting Indians and others while representing his victories to the world? And the feelings he aroused in his audiences, the idealism, the enthusiasm, the excitement, the belief that dreams could become real—must these be declared misguided or a sham because they are associated with the imperialistic conquest of a continent, with the wholesale extermination of animals and men?

It is not so much that we cannot learn from history as that we cannot teach history how things should have been. When I set out to discover how Cody had become involved in the killing of Indians and the slaughter of buffalo, I found myself unable to sustain the outrage I had felt on leaving the museum. From his first job as an eleven-year-old herder for an army supply outfit, sole wage earner for his ailing widowed mother who had a new baby and other children to support, to his death in Colorado at the age of seventy-one, there was never a time when it was possible to say, there, there you went wrong, Buffalo Bill, you should not have killed that Indian. You should have held your fire and made your living some other way and quit the army and gone to work in the nineteenth-century equivalent of the Peace Corps. You should have known how it would end. My reading made me see that you cannot prescribe for someone in Buffalo Bill's position what he should have done, and it made me reflect on how eager I had been to get off on being angry at the museum. The thirst for moral outrage, for self-vindication, lay pretty close to the surface.

I cannot resolve the contradiction between my experience at the Buffalo Bill Historical Center with its celebration of violent conquest and my response to the shining figure of Buffalo Bill as it emerged from the pages of books—on the one hand, a history of shame; on the other, an image of the heart's desire. But I have reached one conclusion that for a while will have to serve.

Major historical events like genocide and major acts of destruction are not simply produced by impersonal historical processes or economic imperatives or ecological blunders; human intentionality is involved and human knowledge of the self. Therefore, if you're really, truly interested in not having any more genocide or killing of animals, no matter what else you might do, if you don't first, or also, come to recognize the violence in yourself and your own anger and your own destructiveness, whatever else you do won't work. It isn't that genocide doesn't matter. Genocide matters, and it starts at home.

"Bill Smith—Number One," by James Bama, 1974. Oil.
Collection of the National Cowboy Hall of Fame and Western Heritage Center,
Oklahoma City, Oklahoma.

The Last of the Breed ☆
Homage to Louis L'Amour

10

I was volunteering temporarily as a file clerk at the Share Our Selves center for services for the poor in Costa Mesa, California. It was one of those dispiriting situations where trying to help people involved dehumanizing them, and yourself; there seemed no way around it. In this case the clients, people in need of food and money and in some cases shelter, sat in rows in a windowless room and waited for their names to be called—Martinez, Rodriguez—so they could receive a bag of groceries or, in special instances, see the lady in the back room who gave out money for electric bills and bus fares.

One day, while filing slips of paper so the people from Costa Mesa (which helped support the center) wouldn't get counted with the people from Santa Ana and other municipalities (which didn't), I noticed a man deeply absorbed in a novel. It was *Fort Everglades* by Frank Slaughter, who wrote adventure stories some decades ago. I asked the man if he'd ever read Louis L'Amour. "Oh yes," he said. At the time, L'Amour had died less than a year before. The man paused and said to me glumly, "You know about L'Amour, don't you?" "Yes," I said, and he replied, "Some people should live forever."

The reverence and respect his words conveyed, their spare eloquence and strength of conviction, reminded me of L'Amour's best writing and of the tough-it-out-against-all-odds philosophy his writing stood for. To the man who spoke them—his name was Roland

Bennett—L'Amour was a hero. No difference, finally, between the writer and his work. There's something about L'Amour's work—the solemnity of living and dying that it captures—that makes you want to pay tribute. Especially now that L'Amour himself has gone west of everything. I never would have gotten involved with Westerns if it hadn't been for L'Amour; his books inspired this book, and his spirit runs through it. L'Amour in his way was a great writer; his works spoke and still speak to millions of people. He has had the praise and gratitude of millions, and so he doesn't really need the words of critics. Still, he deserves critical attention, and certainly he rewards it.

Toward the end of his long career, L'Amour wrote a best-selling novel that was not a Western—not set in the American West or in the nineteenth century. It was called *The Last of the Breed*. The novel is a kind of summa of the books L'Amour had written all his life. Containing the elements normally found in Westerns, it removes them from their usual location in time and space and pushes them to an extreme, as if driving the genre to its lair once and for all, closing in for the kill.

The story is about Major Joseph Makatozi of the U.S. Army Air Force, a test pilot shot down by the Russians, who are after information on the latest experimental aircraft. The flyer is captured, imprisoned, and about to be questioned under torture by his nemesis, Colonel Zamatev, when he escapes into the forest; the rest of the novel consists of his trek across Siberia to the Bering Strait, which he intends to cross as his ancestors had done thousands of years before. For Joe Mack, as he is familiarly known, is mostly Indian—part Sioux, part Cheyenne, and part Scots.

I picked up this book because it had been recommended to me by Rick Hanson, a L'Amour fan I talk to sometimes in a homeless shelter in Durham, North Carolina, the state where I live. I'll return to the shelter later because it's connected to my sense of L'Amour as a writer for Americans, homeless and presidents alike. First, though, I want to explain why I'm writing about this novel.

I'd begun *The Last of the Breed* on a flight to California. As airplane reading it was ideal, immediately replacing my other novel, an appealing story about the life of an Appalachian woman, full of lyric prose, the love of nature, grief, longing, women who endured. It was no contest. Every time I had to decide what to read for the next several days, *The Last of the Breed* won hands down. And this continued. When in preparation for a course I was teaching I began reading another book, *The Education of Little Tree* by Forrest Carter, it was the same. This was arguably a great book, the fictional autobiography of a Cherokee boy growing up in Appalachia during the Depression. It was poetic, it was deeply wise, it was eloquent and moving. It didn't have a chance. I was out there in the *taiga* at sixty degrees below zero with Joe Makatozi, trying to stay alive. No way could I be tempted by an Appalachian spring.

Day after day and night after night I followed him up goat tracks, through forests, across frozen rivers, camping in lean-tos cleverly put together out of blow-downs, sheltered under giant spruces, hidden from pursuers and providing some small respite from the cold. I drank black tea (when he had any tea) made from melted snow boiled over a small fire whose smoke no one would detect because it was diffused by tree branches. I ate strips of broiled meat cut from the carcass of his latest kill—a moose, a deer, a bear (I am a vegetarian)—and shivered with him (though *he* never shivered) as he looked out across the vast territories he had yet to cross, snow-covered, mountainous, uninhabited by men. I curled up with him in caves, scraped animal hides for moccasins, sewed goatskin jackets with stiff fingers, let stone-tipped arrows fly at the throats of would-be assassins. I loved it. I would rather be out there with Joe Makatozi, listening for telltale sounds, running swiftly down forest paths at night, crouching in the brush while his enemies passed by all unsuspecting, than doing almost anything else. I'm sorry I finished the novel. Not even Siberia was large enough to satisfy my hunger for these things.

I know that *The Education of Little Tree* is a better book than *The Last of the Breed*, better for me, and better, I should think, for most people I know. It reflects a truer, more helpful vision of the world than L'Amour's novel. When I put *Little Tree* down, I felt reassured that the world is a safe place to be—not because the book avoids pain, death, cruelty, and human meanness, but because its vision embraces these things, making them part of a larger whole. Forrest Carter lets you feel the goodness in nature and in human beings and lets you see that they are connected. Still, though I know I'm in need of this wisdom, when given a choice, it seems, I go for the ordeal, the long-drawn-out desperate effort, the close calls, the staying power of the determined man. I want the thrill and the risk and the satisfaction that comes from striving against odds. I want the fear.

By which I mean I want the sexiness of it, the titillation you get from reading books where excitement is so acute it becomes a physical sensation. It pulls you in against your will and better judgment. Knowing you should be answering mail, sleeping, washing your hair, you read anyway and keep on reading. You want the adrenaline rush, the stirred-up feeling, the sense, not consciously registered but strongly apprehended nonetheless, that your mind is totally absorbed, occupied by a form of experience that originates outside itself: consciousness traveling at speed down a track it can't get free of without a powerful jolt. To be a prisoner of adventure in this way is to be free—free of the present moment with the burden of consciousness it holds.

Fear is the emotion that most often triggers this intense absorption; that is the first lesson I learned from *The Last of the Breed*. When I finished this book I was really scared. Usually, at the end of a L'Amour novel I feel invigorated, ready to tackle any task at hand, because, with the hero, I've just won out over long odds. But in

The Last of the Breed, though it's strongly implied that the hero will finally escape, it's not absolutely certain (and the title, with its double meaning, makes you wonder). The last we see of Joe Mack, he has arranged for a kayak to cross the Bering Strait, and he is about to fight the man who has been tracking him for the entire novel—a bearlike Yakut tribesman named Alekhin, said never to have let a prisoner escape. But instead of giving us the fight we've been waiting for, L'Amour cuts to Colonel Zamatev, the man who had arranged to have Joe Mack shot down in the first place and who has masterminded the yearlong manhunt for him. In the final scene, Zamatev opens a package strangely wrapped in animal skin and sewn together with thongs. It contains the scalp of Alekhin, who was supposed to kill Joe Mack; now we know who has won that one. Included in the package is a note, neatly lettered on birchbark, referring to the contents. It reads:

THIS WAS ONCE A CUSTOM OF MY PEOPLE. IN MY LIFETIME I SHALL TAKE TWO. THIS IS THE FIRST.

These are the novel's last words. I still feel in my stomach the fear they inspired in me when I read them.

What was I afraid of? That the hero wouldn't escape after all? That the kayak wouldn't be waiting and he would have to endure another winter inside the Arctic Circle? No, it was the other way around. I was afraid for Zamatev, whose scalp Joe Mack meant to take when he returned. (I identified with Zamatev when the story unfolded from his point of view.) And I was upset because of what the note revealed about the hero and, by extension, me. This man, whom I had identified with for most of the novel, slept with, ate with, suffered with, thought with, was really a horror. He wasn't just escaping persecution, he wanted blood. Before, his killing of soldiers had seemed necessary for his own survival. This was different. But it was too late to separate from him there at the last moment, to pretend that I didn't write those words on the birchbark. Suddenly I am a scalper, and I will return to the Soviet Union to claim my next victim. This is who I have been all along without knowing it. So I am afraid at the end, afraid for myself as Zamatev, over whose drab shoulder I read the note, and afraid for myself as Joe Mack, the avenger, who will come in his creamy-white goatskin jacket and leggings to slit Zamatev's throat.

The fear I felt at the end of *The Last of the Breed* is an extreme form of the excitement, tinged with apprehension, that accompanies my reading of most Westerns. It exaggerates something that is always there but not clearly seen. You go to a Western for adventure, or rather for the feeling that adventure stimulates, a feeling of being on the edge, at risk, without a guarantee. First the narrow rivulet of fear running inside you that widens or narrows depending on how close the danger is. Then moments of excited dread—dry throat, tingling palms, accelerated heartbeat—the high. Then moments of relief, the body at ease, comforted, letting go. But it's the fear that keeps you on—there, totally in the moment with the hero in his trial. It's what keeps him going, too, makes him build that lean-to, find a way to muffle his horse's hooves, detect the rifle barrel's glint among the rocks. Fear heightens his perceptions and sends him superhuman strength in the hour of need. When he survives, and your muscles relax, you know that you too will survive, because you feel it in your gut. And you feel once more the feeling that you need to feel—I am safe, I am OK, I will not die.

The cycle of fear and release from fear that the reader goes through is an end in itself, enough of a reason for reading the book. The text turns you on, you get off on it. Carried along by the momentum of the plot and the emotions it arouses, you don't have time to notice too much else. Yet there are things to notice. The world of the Western, as of the spy novel, the detective story, the science fiction adventure, is packed with messages. There is never a moment when you aren't being programmed to believe, act, or feel a certain way. The feelings that reading or seeing a Western excites are related to the principal messages it sends. Intended for men primarily, they are messages about what it means to be a successful adult in our society.

Though *The Last of the Breed* is about an American airman shot down on Russian soil, the real opposition in the novel is not between the United States and the Soviet Union but between the life Joe Mack stands for and the lives of all of us. Joe Mack tells his captors that his only allegiance is to his country, for he has no wife, no children, no living kin. But his patriotism is neither national nor racial nor tribal. Joe Mack is a patriot because he lives close to his instincts, close to the land, and close to the spirit of his ancestors. (His bloodlines give him ancestors on three continents—Asia, Europe, and America—the Indians migrating to America from eastern Siberia, the Scots from Europe). He belongs to the past of the species, to the planet, to earth. His enemies, with one exception, are not defined by language or skin color or ethnic affiliation, but by the way they live—as parts of a bureaucracy, a centralized government, and a giant military machine, flesh and spirit trapped inside huge, complicated organizations of men and equipment. They live like us, the slip-filers.

By contrast, Joe Mack is pure purpose and unadulterated will. An atavistic redeemer, without gospel or program, stripped of everything associated with the name of civilization, he comes to rekindle the will. His mission is to return us to zero, to a state of utter purity before the elements, where essence fronts essence, and there is nothing to get in the way. Joe Mack must stay alive in the Siberian forest in the dead of winter with nothing but his hands and feet. No weapons, no tools, no shelter, no clothing, no food, not even a horse or dog for companionship. (Joe Mack has no animal companions because he *is* the animal, hunted and in hiding, dressed in skins, crouching, eating only the flesh of living things.) His being bereft of everything is essential. It burns away all the accumulated garbage of living: material baggage, mental clutter, emotional entanglements. Joe Mack is naked, free of the past's contamination. His deprivation is ecstatic.

This is how it works. When Joe Mack is almost at the end of his journey, he is captured and beaten and escapes once more, to start again with nothing, a struggle L'Amour describes—and you can feel the accumulated momentum of the narrative pushing the pace along—in a passage that is a mini-version of the whole novel:

> Day after day he had slogged along through storm and sun, working his way, mostly by night when there was any night, toward the east. He had camped in the cold, slept on boughs over icy ground. His feet were in terrible shape, and desperately he needed moccasins.
>
> When the emergency rations taken from the Volga [a Soviet automobile] had given out, he had subsisted on marmots, even voles, and occasionally a ptarmigan.
>
> Shortly after he abandoned the Volga the country had been crisscrossed by helicopters and planes, and during most of that time he had huddled in a niche in a clay bank behind some dead poplars and a few straggling willows, a place planes flew over time and again, the searchers never imagining that even a marmot might conceal itself there. For three days he had had nothing to eat; then he caught some fish in a trap he had woven from plant fibers.
>
> Spring was here, and the tundra was aglow with wildflowers. They were flowers found above timberline in his own country. (359)

The sufferings this passage depicts—the bruised feet, the cold, the uncomfortable boughs—are elixir in the cup of life. This and eating ptarmigan, though we may not be sure what ptarmigan is. Not knowing makes it more delicious. And the trap "woven from plant fibers"—a perfect touch—better than catching fish with bare hands would have been, since it shows more craft and ingenuity. Not to mention his hiding under the enemies' noses for three days. He may be cramped and starving, but he has made fools of them again, with their clumsy technology. Give me a marmot-skin moccasin and some dead poplars to hide under any day and I'll be happy. The joy is in the pain and in the prowess.

Even the reward for staying close to nature and needing nothing— the wildflowers—cannot be enjoyed from a pleasant vantage. They must be seen, as they are here, through a film of pain. And they never will be gathered. For renunciation and denial and doing without are the essence of this life, the guarantors of vitality. Joe Mack rubs stolen vodka on his wounds; he doesn't drink any. He lives as close to the bone as it is possible for a human to live and still survive. "He was always cold." The suffering is relentless.

Rick Hanson, the homeless man, loved it. So, I am sure, did President Reagan, who read *Jubal Sackett* (another L'Amour best-seller) while recovering from cancer; he must have had time to read *The Last of the Breed*, now that he is out of office.

What does this mean? I argued before that the ordeal dramatized in L'Amour's fiction satisfies the modern reader's desire for seriousness, for a life where something really is at stake; that the Western is not an escape from reality but an attempt to get as close to the marrow of things as possible. There is something else involved as well. To live only in the moment on nothing but your nerve is like trying to do without a body at all. To press your soul against the windowpane of being and hold it there. Though the Western hero thrives on physical sensations, the thrill of facing death challenges the mind above all. He goes *through* the body to the mind. The faculty of attention, always operating at capacity, at the crucial moments becomes so concentrated that consciousness is all there is, as if one were lifted out of the body entirely and made into pure awareness.

Body and mind operating at capacity, going beyond their limits into moments of self-transcendence—these are the wished-for experiences that motivate adventure narratives, visitations of the sublime. But these brushes with glory, I am convinced, have a double impact on the reader or viewer only one aspect of which is revealed to casual reflection. Heroic narrative instills a spirit of emulation; you can fight the dragon with Beowulf or swell in righteous anger with the Incredible Hulk and feel motivated to go beyond yourself. But these experiences are purchased at a price. The very process that brings the hero and his reader to moments of exquisite excitement and superhuman concentration has, ultimately, a deadening effect. The hero who is pushed beyond his limits again and again eventually loses the capacity to feel. The result is a gradual etiolation of the nerves whose end point, for the Western hero, is foreshadowed in the desert landscape.

I've said that the hero's trial takes place characteristically within a hostile setting and that the hero's physical body seems sometimes to be an emanation of the land. The harshness of that setting as it's represented in *The Last of the Breed* exceeds the normal limit. The cold that dominates the book from beginning to end is the symbol of this harshness and its embodiment as well. The earth is so cold it is numb. Its body cannot feel anymore. Everything is petrified— the needles of the spruces, the moss underfoot, the rivers, the bark of trees, even the sky. Encased in freezing air, nature is made inaccessible by the cold. The hero's traditional bedding down in nature, nestling into the land's breast, is thwarted by the frigid temperatures. The best he can do is burrow in dank caves or huddle under dead poplars. He feels the cold more as the book progresses, and so do we; the primary physical sensation the book offers is the combined pain and lack of pain produced by slowly freezing.

The hero's body imitates the frozenness of the land by becoming progressively less able to register feeling and reaches the condition of flayed stupor achieved when the body has been driven relentlessly by the will. Victory, in *The Last of the Breed*, means becoming insensate—the freezing, a metaphor for the numbness necessary to withstand circumstances so appalling that to *feel* them would be to wipe out consciousness altogether. The representative episode from L'Amour's *Heller with a Gun* with which this study began ends on the note of numbness:

> His mind was empty. He did not think. Only the occasional tug on the lead rope reminded him of the man who rode behind him.
> It was a hard land, and it bred hard men to hard ways. (15)

And this anesthetization of the hero is present in Westerns generally. The ethic of self-denial—denial of the needs of the flesh for warmth and comfort, succor, ease, and pleasure; and denial of the needs of the spirit for companionship, affection, love, dependency, exchange—turns the hero to stone in the end. He becomes the desert butte.

This mortification of feeling—both the need to mortify feeling and the effect of having done so—motivates much of the Western hero's typical behavior: his impassivity, inexpressive features, the monolithic character of his presence, his stunted language and non-conversational style of speaking. It is not only the need to maintain a power position that makes him a silent interlocutor but the absolute necessity of protecting himself from his own pain. The hero's throat is closed because if he were to open it and speak he would risk letting his feelings out; they might rise to the surface and flood his face, and he would "play the baby" as Steve, the Virginian's bosom friend, so feared to do that even in death he withheld any sign of his affection. For speech is attended by a double risk: pain and the shame of showing that you feel it. So silence and numbness are two aspects of the same thing—the fear of feeling—and they reinforce each other. Afraid of what would come out if he opened up, the hero remains mute and, not speaking, eventually loses touch with the springs of feeling. His humanness then begins to suffer a slow death, and the fate he avoided by surviving the ordeal overtakes him from another quarter unaware.

While he was in the army L'Amour was assigned to Camp McCoy in the Upper Peninsula of Michigan to give instruction in winter survival. It was one of the few army assignments for which he felt "thoroughly equipped." He wrote: "I understood the cold. . . . Several times in Oregon I had taken a rifle or a shotgun and gone into the woods in the depth of winter to spend a week or more just knocking about and camping out. Such forays had taught me a great deal about survival in the cold . . . " (*Education of a Wandering Man*, 139, 140). Elsewhere he writes: "As much time as I have spent in cities . . . I liked the wild country the best. Again and again I returned to the desert or the mountains, seeking out the lonely water holes, studying the wildlife, learning to exist on the outer margins" (130).

L'Amour likes the cold, he likes the wild, and he likes to be alone. He finds something to savor in it. The first nonfiction book he read was called *The Genius of Solitude*, and it made a big impression. At the age of fifteen he left school forever. When his classmates were graduating from Jamestown High, in North Dakota, he was buying Kipling's *Departmental Ditties* at Muhammad Dufalkir's bookshop on High Street in Singapore. In his autobiography, *The Education of a Wandering Man*, L'Amour tells a story about loneliness that reveals something of his attitude toward it. A young teacher L'Amour met who thought he wanted to be alone took a job as caretaker of a mine, miles from anywhere. He brought with him a box full of books— Shakespeare, *The Anatomy of Melancholy*, O. Henry's short stories. He lasted two weeks. L'Amour comments:

> The difficulty was that few people know what it means to be absolutely alone. Even fewer know what silence is. Our lives are filled with the coming and going of people and vehicles, so much so that our senses scarcely notice the sounds. . . . Suddenly, here, the man was *alone*. There was no sound. Occasionally, during the day, a hen might cackle, a loosened pebble might rattle down the rocks. Otherwise, nothing. . . . It was not Walden Pond. (42)

L'Amour likes the sound of that loosened pebble, the silence it implies, and the image of profound tedium accentuated by the cackle of a hen. He took the job and stayed. He found it enjoyable.

There is something in the deliberate loneliness of the life L'Amour lets us glimpse in his memoir, the mining claim vigils, the solitary trips in northern forests, the rented rooms near libraries where he holed up to read, that mirrors the Western hero's isolation. Physically comfortless, without close human ties, dedicated to some nameless goal, it is a monastic existence, but without the communitarian aspects of monastic life and apparently without the introspection. This double denial—denial of intimacy either with other people or with one's self—makes the hero's isolation tremendous.

Except for a brief period in the dead of winter, when he associates with some political exiles in a forest camp (and even then he sleeps in a secret lair he's made for himself in the woods), Joe Makatozi spends the entire novel alone. The only human being in vast stretches of wilderness, he is also in a foreign country. Add to this the gelid air that freezes nature's body against him, and his loneliness would seem unendurable. His only relations are with men who want to kill him and whom he wants to kill. He communicates with them, indirectly, through the traces he leaves of his passage over the earth's surface, though typically he leaves no marks, it being a sign of his prowess to leave none. I believe that this image of the hero, isolated, in pain, involved in an endless kill-or-be-killed struggle for existence, reflects and magnifies the emotional reality of many readers' lives. But it is a reality that the hyperbolic action of the story prevents the reader from having to face.

I never feel lonely when reading L'Amour. I'm too busy trying to stay alive. I never think about the fact that this hero has no friends, just temporary allies, no family, only some shadowy people back home or dead. The excitement of hunting or being hunted, of living close to the land, is enough for him, and me. The thrill of the story and the cycle of fear and relief from fear keep the isolation from appearing. And they keep at bay the entire range of feelings that normally arise in the course of any day. The Western's exclusive focus on do-or-die situations doesn't simply represent life without birth and marriage, growing up, finding a place in the world, and growing old; it leaves out all the emotions that are associated with day-to-day living. If you are always fighting off men with guns or trying not to die from thirst in the desert, it isn't possible to entertain other kinds of feelings. As long as you are reading a story where life hangs in the balance, the tremendous pull of the narrative line guarantees that there will be no mental space for anything else.

While exposing you to death the Western insulates you from life, from the mental clutter and emotional turmoil that attend everyday experience. It is not so much the facts of life the story shields you from as their psychological fallout. In this sense, the reader's experience and the hero's go hand in hand. Forced to confront death on a regular basis, the hero steels himself against all emotions and perceptions that do not lead directly to his conquering. Meanwhile, his wounds ache unattended inside. In a parallel fashion, the reader who stares down the barrel of the enemy's gun becomes familiar with the feelings that accompany life-or-death situations, but remains a comparative stranger in his or her own emotional backyard. The hardened-by-suffering hero and the temporarily anesthetized reader are one.

When seen from this vantage, the message that Westerns are sending their audiences seems to center on the need for numbness. Over and over again in countless Westerns we watch the hero swallow his feelings in order to carry out his difficult and distasteful tasks. The numbing process gathers momentum in post-Western cop narratives like the Dirty Harry series, where the hero has to kill so much he becomes a zombielike extension of his hypertrophied gun; and it ends in robotization in science fiction extensions of this line of development such as *The Terminator*, *RoboCop*, and *Total Recall*. But I never realized how central the process of anesthetization was to establishing the hero's claim to heroism until seeing Anthony Mann's aptly titled *Man of the West* (1958), where the main character, played by Gary Cooper, kills almost every other character in the film, performing progressively more terrible acts until in the end he is completely dehumanized. Repeatedly this character finds himself in situations where, we are supposed to believe, he has no choice but to kill or hurt another person, though in doing so he must quell his humanitarian instincts. In the last scene, when the female lead tells him that she loves him and he meets her declaration with stony silence, he has become incapable of any relationship at all.

What is especially revealing about this film is the expression on

Gary Cooper's face as he performs his deadly duties. It is the characteristic Gary Cooper grimace—the same one he wears all the way through *High Noon*—a compound of pain, disgust, and determination: pain at the horror of what he has to do, disgust at the venality of his fellow humans for forcing him to do it, and determination to do it anyway, despite his softer feelings. His face, twisted so often into this expression, is the visible sign of his condition, of the fallenness of the world he inhabits, of his own distance from and implication in its fallenness, and of how much it hurts him to do what he has to do.

The expression is also the sign that he is not completely callous, not totally inured to the brutality he witnesses and shares in against his will. For what distinguishes the hero from the villains in a Western is that *he still feels* despite all the horror he has seen and all the horror he has perpetrated. In fact, that is how we know he is tough in the way a hero has to be, for his face shows that he has had to harden himself against his own feelings. His heart is not dead; it is battered and bruised inside the casing of his chest. This, his bruised and bleeding heart, hidden behind his leathery exterior and signaled only by the grimness of his face, his heart which is never heard to utter any sound, is what he carries with him back into the wilderness at the end. It is his sacrifice, bound and smoking on the altar of his principles, the thing without which what he did would have no weight at all.

The death of the heart, or, rather, it's scarification and eventual sacrifice, is what the Western genre, more than anything else, is about. The numbing of the capacity to feel, which allows the hero to inflict pain on others, requires the sacrifice of his own heart, a sacrifice kept hidden under his toughness, which is inseparable from his heroic character. Again, at this point, we come upon one of the underlying continuities that link Westerns to the sentimental domestic novels that preceded them. For the hero, who offers himself as a savior of his people, sacrificing his heart so that they can live, replicates the Christian ideal of behavior, giving the self for others, but in a manner that is distorted and disguised so that we do not recognize it. Outwardly the Western hero is the opposite of the sacrificial lamb: he fights, he toughs it out, he seeks the showdown. Instead of dying, he rides out of town alive, a strong man, stronger than the rest, strong enough to do what the others couldn't (kill somebody), strong enough to take his perpetual exile. But inwardly the hero has performed a sacrifice—an ironic and a tragic sacrifice—for the very thing he offers up, his heart, his love, his feelings, are what Christ in the trinitarian division of labor has come to represent. It is also the feminine part of himself, the part that opens him to intimate relations to other people, the part that "plays the baby."

Having renounced his heart so that others might keep theirs (even his physique betrays the truth, the slouch from head to hip, chest concave where the heart had been), he rides away alone. And he must do this not because he is a murderer and therefore not to be trusted, but because having hardened himself to do murder, he can no longer open his heart to humankind. His love is aborted, cut off. When I think of the hero in this way, when I think of Shane or Thomas Dunson or Ethan Edwards, the tough lonely men who lord it over others in countless films, my throat constricts. So much pain sustained internally and denied. So much suffering not allowed to speak its name. When he rides out of town at the end, the hero bears his burdens by himself. When I think of how he feels, no words coming out, everything closed inside, the internal bleeding, the sadness of the genre is terrible, and I want to cry. Instead of emulation or outrage, it's compassion the hero deserves, and compassion alone. I would not trade places with him for anything.

Two Men

11

One night last spring, in the homeless shelter where I volunteer, I talked to Santos Solis, known among the men as "Chief." An Apache from the San Carlos Reservation in Arizona, Santos is an avid fan of Louis L'Amour and knows the hundred-odd novels practically by heart. He told me he was leaving the next day to go home because they were having an election for tribal chief (he's a Chiricahua Apache), and some of his relatives wanted him to run. I asked him if wanted to be chief. "No," he said. "I like roaming around." He told me that he'd been roaming around all his life. He owned a house and a business (a bar) in Idaho, and used to own a restaurant, too, but didn't like the restaurant so he sold it after a while. His wife and three kids were out there, he said, and he went back from time to time, but didn't really like to work in the bar. He preferred the nearby ranches with horses and cattle.

When I asked him how long he'd been roaming, he said when he was eight his mother had married again. She and her new husband moved to Texas and took him along, but he ran away. He'd ended up on a farm where the farmer caught deer and kept them in a pen with a wire fence. Santos had cut the fence to let the deer out, and the farmer had called the police, who came after him. He started running through the cornfield, and they saw him, so he ducked down and crawled along; then he saw them on the road ahead of him, so he turned the other way. And finally, by running and ducking down and turning and going the other way, he got to the woods and escaped. He made it back to Arizona.

I asked him how he'd lived, how he'd eaten. And he said he'd been raised by his grandfather, who had taught him the old ways, that he could get along and didn't need anything. I asked whether he didn't need some implements or tools of some kind, and he said no, he could build traps with his hands. And he could still do it now.

Santos was about to leave for Arizona, but all he had was a bus ticket to Asheville. Some of the men in the shelter asked him why, since he had money in the bank, he didn't just take some out. "When I put money in the bank it stays there," he said. "It's not for takin' out. It's for when I get too old to work. And besides, I came here on a bus from Alabama, and before that I hitchhiked to Alabama from Idaho, and that's the way I'm goin' home."

He looked good, Santos did, tan and healthy. But I asked him how his health was because he'd been sick a few weeks back. He said his health was very good. I said I was just checking, since he was setting out on a journey and all. He said, "What d'ya think, I didn't get to be this old by bein' stupid!" We both laughed.

His Indian name was Wildfire. When I remarked, "Oh, there's a novel by Zane Grey by that name. Did you ever read it?" he said, "Sure, I read all the novels of Zane Grey before I discovered Louis [he pronounced it Lewis] L'Amour."

Santos had engaged me in conversation that night by asking me if I remembered the date of L'Amour's death. I said I thought it had been in the fall of '88. "No," he said, "it was June." We'd had some discussion about this before. When he'd gotten his suitcase back after being without it for a while (he must have been storing it somewhere; it's hard for the men to keep things in the shelter) he told me the first thing he went for was his news clipping of L'Amour's obituary. It said L'Amour had died on the tenth of June 1988, though it wasn't reported in the newspapers until the following Monday.

Santos cares about this date more than I do, even though I write about L'Amour, because for him L'Amour was more than a subject for contemplation, more than an author. He'd read all of L'Amour's novels five times. He had spent a lot of time in the world L'Amour invented. He knew it well, had lived it in his mind, and had also seen it and lived it in his life. Santos, like L'Amour, had been a wandering man and, like L'Amour and Grey, seemed to be one of those for whom the relation between reading and living was incredibly close.

Near the end of *The Last of the Breed*, L'Amour writes of the hero: "He walked upon a mountain and saw the sea's reflection in the sky" (363), a sentence that reflects L'Amour's sense of himself and of his relation to the world. For the man in the sentence, nothing stands between the world and him. He seems to own the world in that he controls his own experience of it. There was something of that conviction in Santos. He delivered his statements about the world with a certainty that defied contradiction. L'Amour's sentence also contains the ring of finality and achievement that accompany the successful completion of a task, for it marks the moment when Joe Makatozi has finally reached the sea. "He walked upon a mountain" has that world-historical feeling you get from history books that talk about men who helped to "build a nation," and it has the epic note L'Amour strikes when writing about his fiction ("I sing of arms and men"). This man, the epic-historical man, the man of the sentence who controls the world he beholds, is *the* man, the one who stands for all. When you read a L'Amour novel, you step into this man's shoes.

Can this be why L'Amour was a favorite author of a president and three men I happened to meet in homeless shelters, Santos Solis, Rick Hanson, and Roland Bennett?

I know that at least one of these men, Santos, is fairly well satisfied with his life. He bivouacked in the shelter because he didn't want a more permanent arrangement. He took food for himself and some to feed the birds. He was never drunk. He held regular outdoor jobs. The night before he left for Asheville and points west, he was fit, trim, dressed in jeans and a nice shirt and a modified cowboy hat with a leather tassel, an orange feather, and a turquoise-colored decoration. I have always felt sure he made it back to Arizona.

The other person I know who loved L'Amour novels was my father-in-law, Max Fish. A Jewish immigrant from Poland who came over at the age of fifteen, he learned English in public school and then went to work for his uncle (whom he hated) as a plumber's apprentice, carrying bathtubs on his back. After he married and had a child and the war came, he wanted to go into business for himself, but his uncle wouldn't help him. So he borrowed the money for his license and a set of tools and did it anyway. When he retired, he was the largest plumbing contractor in southern New England.

I felt that in many respects Max was like a L'Amour hero. Life had been tough for him, but he endured. I remember one evening while we were eating at a restaurant, he told a story about leaving Poland. There had been a gang of boys in his village, Gentiles, who used to beat him up because he was a Jew. One in particular was a terrible bully. The day before he left for America, Max came upon this boy alone and attacked him. He beat him badly and left him lying on the ground. He never found out whether the boy had lived or died. Max told this story with a mixture of pain and resentment, awe at himself, and satisfaction tinged with horror. He hadn't forgotten the pain of those beatings yet.

Something in this story made me understand my father-in-law better. He was a silent man, massively built, with a face like hammered bronze: strong, weathered, tan, with small blue-green eyes that sometimes resembled chips of ice. A powerful presence. He was the family savior, godfather type. When somebody got into trouble, they came to Max. His behavior in these cases was always a mixture of shrewdness and generosity. He brought relatives over from Israel, found housing for them, got them jobs. Other relatives he set up in business; still others he hired at his own firm until they were able to get work elsewhere. You knew that if you ever really needed something, he'd be there. He was a doer, practical in every molecule of his body. He was a rock.

I never figured out what the range of his sensitivities was. Sometimes he was deep and subtle in his understanding of other people, kind and simple in his actions. Sometimes he seemed not to see, not to hear, not to care what other people felt.

He wanted you to know that he was not a man people could put things over on. This was often the point of the stories he told at social gatherings when he broke his usual silence and entertained the group with perfectly timed accounts of his exploits. In these stories Max bested his adversaries through acts of superior cunning and bravado, based on a fund of negotiating experience, hard common sense, and excellent judgment. The stories were punctuated by moments of extraordinary selflessness on his part, an ability to cut his losses as if they had never existed, to sustain insult without taking the least offense. As a character, he kept you on tenterhooks the way he did in his stories. Will he sock you one? Ignore you? Or offer you the moon? He never did any of these things where I was concerned, but there was something in his bearing that created such expectations and kept them alive.

Max had no opinions to offer about L'Amour. He liked to read the novels but said this in a slightly deprecating way. He found them entertaining, something to pass the time, I wasn't to make too much of it. Yet I think he'd read almost all of the hundred-odd books L'Amour wrote.

Why? I don't know. But I do know that there was something in Max and in Santos Solis that I recognized: a certain hardness, a willingness to decide, to act without mercy and without regret. Qualities necessary in the Western hero, and which, because I feel so little capable of them, I admire. There was a philosophical attitude implicit in the way both Santos and my father-in-law approached life, an acceptance of fate underlying the need for control which seemed to put them beyond right and wrong and suggested the irrelevance of judgment. They saw themselves impersonally, as if part of some cliff's rocky face. It is here that I would like to leave them, along with John Wayne and Thomas Dunson and Ethan Edwards, Lassiter, the Man of the West, Gary Cooper in *High Noon*, Shane, Wyatt Earp, and all the rest.

Still from *McKenna's Gold* (Columbia, 1969).
Courtesy of the Museum of Modern Art/Film Stills Archive, New York.

Epilogue ☆
Fighting Words

When it shows up in Westerns, we think we know what violence is: it's the shoot-out on Main Street at the end of the movie, and the fistfight or two that precede it. It's what Amy, played by Grace Kelly in *High Noon*, is protesting against when she says, just before Gary Cooper has his duel with Frank Miller's gang: "I don't care who's right or who's wrong. There has to be some better way for people to live!" The definition of violence most of us carry around in our heads differs very little from the one the Western offers: violence is killing or beating up on other people, deliberately inflicting pain. The rifle that misfires can kill violently, but that's not the kind of thing we're concerned with when we think about violence as a moral issue. Intention has to be involved.

Working on Westerns has made me aware of the extent to which the genre exists in order to provide a justification for violence. Violence needs justification because our society puts it under interdict—morally and legally, at any rate. In *Shane*, for example, when Shane first appears at Grafton's store, he goes into the saloon section and buys a bottle of soda pop. One of the Riker gang (the villains in this movie) starts insulting him, first saying he smells pigs (Shane is working for a farmer), then ridiculing him for drinking soda pop, then splashing a shot of whiskey on his brand new shirt with the words "smell like a man," and finally ordering him out of the saloon. Shane goes quietly. But the next time, when he returns the empty soda bottle and the insults start again, he's had enough. When Shane is told he can't "drink with the men," he splashes whiskey in the other guy's face, hauls off and socks him one, and the fight is on.

The structure of this sequence reproduces itself in a thousand Western novels and movies. Its pattern never varies. The hero, provoked by insults, first verbal, then physical, resists the urge to retaliate, proving his moral superiority to those who are taunting him. It is never the hero who taunts his adversary; if he does, it's only after he's been pushed "too far." And this, of course, is what always happens. The villains, whoever they may be, finally commit an act so atrocious that the hero *must* retaliate in kind. He wants to, and we want him to, and, if there's a crowd of innocent by-standers, they want him to, too. At this juncture, the point where provocation has gone too far, retaliatory violence becomes not sim-ply justifiable but imperative: now, we are made to feel, *not* to transgress the interdict against violence would be the transgression.

Why does the Western tell this story over and over? This is not a question I am prepared to answer fully, but one or two things can be said. There's no denying the satisfying sense of release the plot's culmination in violence affords. The entire purpose of the pattern I've described is to get the audience to the point where it can't wait till the hero lets loose with his six-shooters. (In fact, the culminating moment is not always—or perhaps even usually—one of letting go: the actual movements involved, the facial expressions, the bodily positions, are not those of all-out effort or abandon but of taut control.) Still, there's a tremendous feeling of relief at the moment of discharge, relief from the tension that holding back the urge to strike has built up. Vengeance, by the time it arrives, feels biolog-ically necessary. It's as if the hero had been dying of thirst, and suddenly he's given the chance to take a drink of water; it's as if he's been waiting eight and a half innings to come up to bat.

Whatever the appropriate analogy is (the most common one is sexual) the violence, by the time it arrives, fills a visceral need.

Mixed with the pleasure of this moment is another, less noted, for it tends to become submerged in the fury of physical appeasement. The story can climax, and desire be sated, only if the moral applause meter reads way off the scale in the hero's favor. What justifies his violence is that he is in the right, which is to say that he has been unduly victimized and can now be permitted to do things which a short while ago only the villains did. At this moment, a flip-flop occurs. Virtue, which up till then had shown itself in long-suffering and restraint, is suddenly transformed and now consists of all-out aggression. This is the moment of moral ecstasy. The hero is *so right* (that is, so wronged) that he can kill with impunity. And we are with him one hundred percent. The feeling of supreme righteousness in this instant is delicious and hardly to be distinguished from murderousness. I would almost say they are the same thing.

I want to switch now to a different mise-en-scène: an academic conference, where a woman is giving a paper. It is an attack on another woman's recent book; the entire paper is devoted to demolishing it, and the speaker is doing a superb job. The audience has begun to catch the spirit of the paper, which is witty, elegant, pellucid, and razor sharp; they appreciate the deftness, the brilliance, the grace with which the assassination is being conducted; the speaker's intelligence flatters their intelligence, her taste becomes their taste, her principles their principles. They start to laugh at the jokes. They are inside the paper now, pulling with the speaker, seeing her victim in the same way she does, as the enemy, as someone whose example should be held up to scorn because her work is pernicious and damaging to the cause. (For my purposes here, it doesn't matter what the cause is, what the speaker was right about, or what sins the victim was guilty of.)

Listening to the paper, which I admired very much for the performance values I've mentioned, I began to feel more and more uncomfortable. The more the audience pulled with the speaker, the more I shrank away. The sensation I felt was fear. I was afraid that this woman might someday turn her attack on me—indeed, in one of her devastating sideswipes, I thought I had already been anonymously grazed by her dagger—and I imagined the audience, which only the day before had enthusiastically applauded my own presentation, turning on me like a pack of dogs. By the time the paper was over, I felt as if I had been present at a ritual execution of some sort, something halfway between a bullfight, where the crowd admires the skill of the matador and enjoys his triumph over the bull, and a public burning, where the crowd witnesses the just punishment of a criminal. For the academic experience combined the elements of admiration, bloodlust, and moral self-congratulation.

Afterward, I began to recall in a kind of phantasmagoria all the essays I had read where similar executions had occurred. It wasn't the essays themselves that came to mind as much as the moves they characteristically made. The audience, a moment ago, had laughed loudest when the victim's stylistic gaffes were held up to scorn, and I remembered the times I had seen someone's diction ridiculed or their unhappy choice of metaphor derided. I remembered the shapes of dismemberment: occasions when the absurd consequences of the victim's arguments were displayed for all to see, the innumerable times people had been garrotted by their own self-contradictions. But most vivid of all were the moments when the characterological defects implicit in someone's style or point of view were indignantly paraded by. Following traditional lines of thought was translated into cowardice, dependence on another scholar's work into toadyism, failing to mention another critic's work into lack of generosity, and so on. The list is practically endless. In veiled language, I realized, we accuse one another of stupidity, ignorance, fear, envy, pride, malice, and hypocrisy; we picture those with whom we disagree as monsters of inhumanity and manage to insinuate that they lack social graces as well as social conscience and moral virtue; we hint that they are insensitive, pompous, narrow, affected, shrill, exhibitionistic, and boring. We feel justified in exposing these errors to view, that they may be scourged not in the sight of God, since no god presides over modern warfare, but in the sight of our professional peers and superiors. We feel justified in this because we are right, so right, and they, like the villains in the Western, are wrong, so wrong.

Lost thus in amazement at the venality of my fellow human beings, I remembered something else, an essay I had published in 1981 that, twice anthologized since then, had been in many ways the making of my career. Strange that such an essay should pop to mind. And then I realized: the essay began with a frontal assault on another woman scholar. When I wrote it I felt the way the hero does in a Western. Not only had this critic argued *a*, *b*, and *c*, she had held *x*, *y*, and *z*! It was a clear case of outrageous provocation. Moreover, she was famous and I was not. She was teaching at a prestigious university and I was not. She had published a major book and I had not. In this David and Goliath situation—my slingshot against her ca(n)non—surely I was justified in hitting her with everything I had. And so, casting myself as champion of the oppressed, and wielding scare quotes and withering sarcasm, I showed the world the evil of her ways and out of the shambles of her position went on to build the temple of my own. The actual onslaught only lasted a page and a half, but the sense of outrage that produced it fueled me as I wrote the entire essay; sometimes I would even reopen her book to get back my sense of passionate conviction.

The showdown on Main Street isn't the prerogative of the Western; it's not the special province of men (as opposed to women); or of popular culture as opposed to literary criticism. Television cop shows, *Rambo*, and *Dirty Harry*, and their fans do not occupy a different moral universe from the one populated by academicians. Violence takes place in the conference rooms at scholarly meetings and in the pages of professional journals; and although it's not the same thing to savage a person's book as it is to kill them with a six-gun, I suspect that the nature of the feelings that motivate both acts is qualitatively the same. This bloodless kind of violence that takes place in our profession is not committed by other people; it's practiced at some time or other by virtually everyone. "Have gun, will travel" is just as fitting a theme for academic achievers as it was for Paladin.

These remarks could be expanded considerably and their implications variously drawn out. It would be possible, for instance, to look at what I've said within the context of entrepreneurial capitalism, which presumably creates an incentive and framework for both sorts of confrontational behavior I've been describing, the Western hero's and the academician's. Or the scenario could be explained institutionally, and the competitive nature of academic professionalism blamed for the patterns of conduct chronicled here. But although I think it would be fruitful to examine such circumstantial constraints, I find myself focusing inward, drawn back to the moment when I returned to my adversary's text for replenishment. I did so because I knew instinctively that it would sharpen my mind, energize my body, strengthen my will—in short, that it would restore vigor and momentum to my argument. In order to go on, I needed to feel again the moment when the villains go too far, the moment of righteous wrath that sweeps everything else away. At that precise instant, something inside says, "charge." It is an experience of tremendous empowerment. You feel invincible. All the faculties are galvanized, perfectly aligned, ready to do your will. It's the moment to look out for, the karmic moment.

These remarks have a moralizing tendency, to say the least, and at this juncture it would seem I ought to say something like, "And so the cowboys and the farmers should be friends," or "Do unto other critics as you would have other critics do unto you." I believe in peace and I believe in the Golden Rule, but I don't believe I've earned the right to such pronouncements. At least not yet. It's difficult to unlearn the habits of a lifetime, and this very essay has been fueled by a good deal of the righteousness it is in the business of questioning. So instead of offering you a moral, I call your attention to a moment: the moment of righteous ecstasy, the moment when you know you have the moral advantage of your adversary, the moment of murderousness. It's a moment when there's still time to stop, there's still time to reflect, there's still time to recall what happened in *High Noon*, there's still time to say, "I don't care who's right or who's wrong. There has to be some better way for people to live."

Works Cited

Western Movies

Angel and the Bad Man (1946, Republic). Director: James Edward Grant.
Ballad of Cable Hogue, The (1969, Warner Brothers). Director:
      Sam Peckinpah.
Big Country, The (1958, United Artists). Director: William Wyler.
Butch Cassidy and the Sundance Kid (1969, Fox). Director: George Roy Hill.
Cheyenne Autumn (1964, Warner Brothers). Director: John Ford.
Cowboy (1958, Columbia). Director: Delmer Daves.
Cowboys, The (1972, Warner Brothers). Director: Mark Rydell.
Dakota Incident (1956, Republic). Director: Lewis Foster.
Dances with Wolves (1990, Orion). Director: Kevin Costner.
Destry Rides Again (1939, Universal). Director: George Marshall.
Duel in the Sun (1946, Independent). Director: King Vidor.
Gunfight at the OK Corral (1957, Paramount). Director: John Sturges.
High Noon (1952, United Artists). Director: Fred Zinnemann.
High Plains Drifter (1973, Universal). Director: Clint Eastwood.
Hour of the Gun (1967, United Artists). Director: John Sturges.
Jesse James (1939, Fox). Director: Henry King.
Johnny Guitar (1954, Republic). Director: Nicholas Ray.
Lonely Are the Brave (1962, Universal). Director: David Miller.
Man Called Horse, A (1969, National General Pictures). Director:
      Elliot Silverstein.

Man of the West (1958, United Artists). Director: Anthony Mann.

Man Without a Star (1955, Universal). Director: King Vidor.

Monte Walsh (1970, National General Pictures). Director: William A. Fraker.

My Darling Clementine (1946, Fox). Director: John Ford.

One-Eyed Jacks (1960, Paramount). Directors: George Cukor and
    Marlon Brando.

100 Rifles (1969, Fox). Director: Tom Gries.

Outlaw Josey Wales, The (1976, Warner Brothers). Directors: Clint Eastwood
    and Philip Kaufman.

Red River (1948, United Artists). Director: Howard Hawks.

Rio Bravo (1959, Warner Brothers). Director: Howard Hawks.

Rio Grande (1950, Republic). Director: John Ford.

Santa Fe Trail (1940, Warner Brothers). Director: Michael Curtiz.

Searchers, The (1956, Warner Brothers). Director: John Ford.

Shane (1953, Paramount). Director: George Stevens.

She Wore a Yellow Ribbon (1949, RKO Radio Pictures). Director: John Ford.

Shootist, The (1976, Paramount). Director: Don Siegel.

Stagecoach (1939, United Artists). Director: John Ford.

Texas (1941, Columbia). Director: George Marshall.

True Grit (1969, Paramount). Director: Henry Hathaway.

Wagonmaster (1950, RKO Radio Pictures). Director: John Ford.

Warlock (1959, Fox). Director: Edward Dmytryk.

Wild Bunch, The (1969, Warner Brothers). Director: Sam Peckinpah.

Will Penny (1968, Paramount). Director: Tom Gries.

Winchester '73 (1950, Universal). Director: Anthony Mann.

Western Novels

Grey, Zane. *Betty Zane* (New York: Charles Francis Press, 1903).

———. *The Last of the Plainsmen* (New York: The Outing Publishing
    Company, 1908).

———. *The Heritage of the Desert* (New York: Harper & Brothers, 1910).

———. *Riders of the Purple Sage*, ed. Jane Tompkins. (New York: Penguin
    Books, 1990; first published by Harper & Brothers, 1912).

———. *The Light of Western Stars* (New York: Harper & Row, 1914).

———. *Wanderer of the Wasteland* (New York: Harper & Row, 1923).

L'Amour, Louis. *Hondo* (New York: Bantam Books, 1953).

———. *Heller with a Gun* (Greenwich, Conn.: Fawcett, 1955).

———. *Silver Canyon* (London: Bouregy & Curl, 1956).

———. *Radigan* (New York: Bantam Books, 1958).

———. *Sackett* (New York: Bantam Books, 1961).

———. *High Lonesome* (New York: Bantam Books, 1962).

———. *Galloway* (New York: Bantam Books, 1970).

———. *Treasure Mountain* (New York: Bantam Books, 1972).

———. *The Lonesome Gods* (New York: Bantam Books, 1983).

———. *Jubal Sackett* (New York: Bantam Books, 1985).

———. *The Last of the Breed* (New York: Bantam Books, 1986).

Wister, Owen. *The Virginian*, ed. Sidney Clark. (New York: Heritage Press, 1951; first published by Macmillan, 1902).

———. *Lady Baltimore* (New York: Macmillan, 1906).

———. *Lin McLean* (New York: A. L. Burt, 1907).

———. A Wise Man's Son, unpublished manuscript.

Other Sources

Bell, Malcolm, Jr. *Major Butler's Legacy: Five Generations of a Slaveholding Family*. Athens: University of Georgia Press, 1987.

Cawelti, John G. *Adventure, Mystery, and Romance: Formula Stories as Art and Popular Culture*. Chicago: University of Chicago Press, 1976.

———. *The Six-Gun Mystique*. 2nd ed. Bowling Green, Ohio: Bowling Green State University Popular Press, 1984.

Cody, Iron Eyes. *Iron Eyes: My Life as a Hollywood Indian*, as told to Collin Perry. New York, Everest House, 1982.

Degler, Carl. *At Odds: Women and the Family in America from the Revolution to the Present*. New York: Oxford University Press, 1980.

Dobie, J. Frank. *The Mustangs*. Boston: Little, Brown, 1934.

Etulain, Richard. "Origins of the Western." *Critical Essays on the Western American Novel*, ed. William T. Pilkington. Boston: G. K. Hall, 1980.

Gallagher, Tag. *John Ford: The Man and His Films*. Berkeley: University of California Press, 1986.

Grey, Zane. "Breaking Through." *American Magazine* 98 (July 1924): 11–13, 76–80.

———. "What the Desert Means to Me." *American Magazine* 98 (November 1924): 5–8, 72–78.

Gruber, Frank. *Zane Grey: A Biography*. New York: World Publishing Co., 1970.

Hite, Shere. *The Hite Report: Women and Love—A Cultural Revolution in Progress*. New York: Knopf, 1987.

Hymowitz, Carol, and Michaele Weissman. *A History of Women in America*. New York: Bantam Books, 1978.

Jackson, Carlton. *Zane Grey*. New York: Twayne Publishers, 1973.

Kolodny, Annette. *The Land Before Her: Fantasy and Experience of the American Frontiers, 1930–1860*. Chapel Hill: University of North Carolina Press, 1984.

Lamar, Howard R., ed. *The Reader's Encyclopedia of the American West*. New York: Crowell, 1977.

L'Amour, Louis. *Education of a Wandering Man*. New York: Bantam, 1989.

Miller, Alice. *For Your Own Good: Hidden Cruelty in Child-Rearing and the Roots of Violence*. New York: Farrar, Straus, Giroux, 1983.

Nachbar, John G. *Western Films: An Annotated Critical Bibliography*. New York: Garland, 1975.

Payne, Darwin. *Owen Wister: Chronicler of the West, Gentleman of the East*. Dallas: Southern Methodist University Press, 1985.

Russell, Donald B. *The Lives and Legends of Buffalo Bill*. Norman, Okla.: University of Oklahoma Press, 1960.

Schwenger, Peter. *Phallic Critiques*. London: Routledge & Kegan Paul, 1984.

Van Dyke, John C. *The Desert*. Salt Lake City: Peregrine Smith, 1980.

Vicinus, Martha. *Suffer and Be Still: Women in the Victorian Age*. Bloomington: Indiana University Press, 1972.

Ward, Benedicta. *The Desert Christian: Sayings of the Desert Fathers*. New York: Macmillan, 1975.

Weybright, Victor, and Henry Blackman Sell. *Buffalo Bill and the Wild West*. New York: Oxford University Press, 1955.

Wister, Owen. "The Evolution of the Cow-Puncher." *Harper's Monthly* 91 (September 1895): 602–17.

Wright, Will. *Six Guns and Society: A Structural Study of the Western*. Berkeley: University of California Press, 1975.

Yost, Nellie Snyder. *Buffalo Bill, His Family, Friends, Fame, Failure, and Fortunes*. Chicago: Sage Books, 1979.

Index

RoboCop, 218
Rocky Mountain, 46
Rogers, Roy, 5, 15, 100, 112
Roosevelt, Theodore (Teddy), 27, 28, 37, 187, 189
Roth, Lina Elise. *See* Grey, Lina Elise
Russell, Charles M., 88
Russell, Don, 199–201
Ryan, Robert, 18

Salvation, 13
Santa Fe Trail, The, 49
Schwenger, Peter, 55–56
Science, 34
Searchers, The, 8, 9, 40–41, 49, 52, 54, 69
Self, 175; animal or child, 122–23, 149, 151–54, 198, 200, 220; -control, 66, 75–76, 175; -deception, 175; -denial, 214–15, 217; difficulty of defining, 112–13; landscape and hero's sense of, 81, 168–71; -transcendence, 76, 213; -transformation, 4, 137; transported, 161–62; unconsciousness of, 56–58. *See also* Hero
Sell, Henry Blackman, 201
Sentimental novel, 37–39, 125–26, 174, 219. *See also* Domesticity
Sentimentality, conventional view of, 120–21
Sex, 60–61, 82, 84, 139, 169–70, 175, 177
Shakespeare, William, 55, 216
Shane, 5, 8, 51–52, 61–62, 127–28, 143, 220, 225, 227–28
She Wore a Yellow Ribbon, 8
Sheldon, Charles M., 28–31, 34, 37, 69, 72
Shootist, The, 25–27
Shoot-out as substitute for matrimony, 35
Short, Luke, 5
Sienkiewicz, Hendryk, 30
Silence: as domination, 59–60; of men, 61–63; numbness and, 214–15, 219; women's and men's, 64. *See also* Hero; Language; Numbness; Words
Silver (horse), 16, 89, 98–100
Singer, Isaac Bashevis, 118
Slaughter, Frank, 205
Social home-making, 42–43. *See also* Domesticity
Solis, Santos, 221–23, 225

Stagecoach, 57, 68–69
Starface (horse), 103–4
Starrett, Joe and Marian, 61–62, 128, 143
Stevens, Wallace, 27
Stewart, Jimmy, 34
Stowe, Harriet Beecher, 37–38
Strength, 34, 51
Suffering: of animals, 119; attraction to, 19; of heroes, 104–6. *See also* Pain

Technology, science and, 34, 177
Ten-gallon hat, 197, 200
Terminator, The, 218
Texas, 69
Things, words and, 48
Tombstone (town), 24, 25, 66
Tonto, 16, 98–100. *See also* Indians
Tony (horse), 100.
Tory, "Stonewall," 52
Total Recall, 218
Town, landscape, hero, and, 85–87
Trigger (horse), 100, 112
True Grit, 50, 124
Trumbo, Dalton, 102
Truth, 31, 52–53; about life, 47–48. *See also* Reality

Urbanization, 43

Van Dyke, John C., 77
Venters, Bern, 32–33, 37, 168, 175
Vicinus, Martha, 126
Victoria (queen of England), 200–201
Violence, 37, 172, 190, 227–33: aestheticization of, 183–84; formalized, 24; intentionality of, 227; legitimization of, 174; male, 28, 144; toward children, 121–22. *See also* Pain; Suffering
Virility, School of, 55–56
Virtue, Christian, 38

Wagonmaster, 8, 90–92
Wallace, Lew, 30
Ward, Benedicta, 83–84
Ward, Mrs. Humphry, 30
Warlock, 8, 25, 35, 105
Warner, Susan, 37–38
Wayne, John, 2, 5, 7, 26, 36, 41, 52–54, 57–58, 62, 65–66, 83, 114, 124, 225
Weissman, Michele, 43
Weybright, Victor, 201
Whitney Gallery of Western Art, 180–85,